the extra-terrestrial's guide to the (X) files

ABOVE TOP SECRET
EYES ONLY
RESTRICTED ACCESS
INQUIRE=DOC10D
ITEM NO=00708805

CLEARE **F.B.I.**
BY CENSOR'S OFFICE
FOR RELEASE 9/9/96

SUBJ: LEIGH, M.C. & LEPINE, M.P. SUBVERSIVE PUBLICATIONS

MARK LEIGH'S interest in the paranormal began when he was ▬▬▬▬ by three small ▬▬▬▬▬▬▬▬▬ while he was ▬▬▬▬ing. Once in their ▬▬▬▬ he was subjected to ▬▬▬▬▬▬ including having a metallic probe inserted into his ▬▬▬▬▬▬, resulting in a ▬▬▬▬▬▬ ▬▬▬▬▬▬ very sore. Subsequent medical examination revealed a higher than normal ▬▬▬▬▬▬ and a ▬▬▬▬▬▬ ▬▬▬▬ very moist. Little is known of his personal life except to say that he lives in SW London, England, with his wife Debbie and children Polly and Barney. He has a large ▬▬▬▬▬.

MIKE LEPINE is 35, British and married with one son. Typical behaviour is amply demonstrated by the occasion upon which said individual ▬▬▬▬▬ ▬▬▬▬ ▬▬▬▬ ▬▬▬▬ ▬▬▬▬ ▬▬▬▬ ▬▬▬▬ ▬▬▬▬ porpoise ▬▬▬▬▬▬ and can never go back to that hotel again. As a security threat, he is rated ▬▬▬▬ almost ▬▬▬▬ ▬▬▬▬, mainly because he can be readily bribed with ▬▬, ▬▬▬▬ and ▬▬ Guides.

LEIGH and LEPINE are known to be responsible for 17 highly subversive books including *How To Be A Complete* ▬▬▬▬, *The Politically Incorrect* ▬▬▬▬▬, *The* ▬▬▬▬▬▬ and the stinging attack upon the British Establishment, *Back to Basics*. Additionally, they have written books for well-known dissidents including ▬▬▬ Edmondson, ▬▬▬ Clary, ▬▬ 'Chubby' ▬▬▬ and Rolf Harris. Their seditious television work has been linked to a wide number of British celebrities including ▬▬ and Pace, Russ ▬▬▬, ▬▬▬ Beadle, Jimmy ▬▬▬ and ▬▬▬▬. Suggest the new series produced by Leigh and Lepine for Discovery, *Would You Believe It?*, be watched closely during 1997.

F.B.I.

PAGE:

SURVEILLANCE PHOTOGRAPH

INQUIRE=DOC 10D
ITEM NO=00708805
SUGGESTED COURSE OF ACTION

▬▬▬▬▬ ▬▬▬▬▬ ▬▬▬▬▬▬
THEIR MOTHERS WOULD ▬▬▬ SO NOT EVEN ▬▬▬▬▬▬ AND ▬▬▬, FOURTEEN DIFFERENT STATES OF THE UNION ▬▬▬ TOES.

R 301259Z SEP 96
FM JOINT STAFF WASHINGTON DC
RUEAIIA/CIA WASHDC
RUEKJCS/SECDEF WASHDC
FM ▬▬▬▬▬▬
RUEHC/SECSTATE WASHDC

the extra-terrestrial's guide to the X files

MARK LEIGH
AND MIKE LEPINE

HEADLINE

First published in 1996
by HEADLINE BOOK PUBLISHING

10 9 8 7 6 5 4 3 2 1

ISBN 0 7472 7744 3

Book interior by Design/Section, Frome

Printed and bound in Great Britain by
Mackays of Chatham PLC, Chatham, Kent

HEADLINE BOOK PUBLISHING
A division of Hodder Headline PLC
338 Euston Road
London NW1 3BH

X-FILE X-50897
COMPUTER REF: ACK/PIC
REPORT BY LEIGH, M.C./LEPINE, M.P.
EYES ONLY

Acknowledgements

Special thanks to Peter Bennett, Rob Ewen,
Gingie, Melanie ('lovely legs') Hammerton, Debbie Leigh,
Edith and Philip Leigh, Philippa Hatton-Lepine,
Harold Lepine, Ian Marshall, Judy Martin, Len Nobbs,
and all the wags at Kirtland AFB.

Illustrations by Terry Carter © 1996.

Picture Credits

Catherine Ashmore: 110; Camera Press: 57T;
Mary Evans Picture Library: 30T; Hulton Deutsch Collection
Limited: 23L & R, 25TL, CR & BR, 37BR, 41, 42, 43, 44, 50, 59, 74, 116;
Kobal Collection: 30B; Popperfoto: 63; Redferns: 56, 57C & B;
Retna: 106, 115, 117, 124, 138; Rex Features: 25BR, 112;
Science Photo Library: 141; Sipa Press: 24R;
Tony Stone Images: 9, 107R; Today: 24L.

INTRODUCTION

I'm going home now. The last 10,000 years have felt more like 30,000 years, as I directed our tasks here in secret on this world. You who follow will discover this for yourselves.

In all my time here, the greatest threat to our operations I encountered was posed by two humans, Fox Mulder and Dana Scully, agents of the law enforcement body called the Federal Bureau of Investigation. They set out to expose us through the instigation of 'The X-Files' project. In return,

we worked tirelessly to undermine them and have the X-Files shut down.

We used the very latest technology, the combined resources of our own operations and human intelligence agencies. We used subterfuge. We used trickery. We used mind control. We used the gene vats. We used clones. We used Michael J. Fox (but he wasn't much use and so doesn't appear in the pages which follow). We used Presidents, abductees and items of furniture. In the end though, things turned out the way they did primarily because of sheer good luck: the man running the X-Files was a complete fruit loop...

F.B.I.

```
NAME: Fox William Mulder
RANK: Special Agent
BADGE: JTT047101111
CURRENT ASSIGNMENT: Project Head - X-Files
IMMEDIATE SUPERVISOR: Assistant Director Walter S. Skinner
```

PERFORMANCE ASSESSMENT - STRICTLY PRIVATE AND CONFIDENTIAL

PREPARED BY SPECIAL AGENT DANA SCULLY FOR SECTION CHIEF BLEVINS, VCU.

Fox Mulder is an extremely dedicated agent, who will go to any lengths to resolve a case, even when to do so requires using extremely unorthodox means.

While his dedication is unquestionable, he has displayed a keenness to accept evidence and a preference for 'unconventional' answers rather than more rational explanations, which sometimes might be termed 'obsessive'. This may stem from the disappearance of his younger sister, Samantha, in his childhood which he attributes to 'alien abduction'.

The personality problems reported by Agent Cooper during the 'Black Lodge' case up at Twin Peaks have shown no signs of resurfacing, and I confidently predict we have seen the last of 'Denise'.

Putting Mulder in charge of the X-Files - FBI cases with a high degree of strangeness - was probably not, in retrospect, the wisest of personnel decisions, since he finds it difficult to exercise the objectivity required in cases containing what appear to be elements of the paranormal. See over for examples:

X-FILE X-71112
MULDER'S CONCLUSION: 'The Mayan prophecies – and the dire warning contained in the geometry of the Great Pyramid – are about to be realised. A new Ice Age is upon us.'
ACTUAL CASE SOLUTION: Faulty air conditioning.

X-FILE X-72312
MULDER'S CONCLUSION: 'Things are the same, but subtly different. Perhaps only a trained investigator's eye would spot it. The FBI building is not the same one I left on Friday. I can only offer one of two explanations. Either some illicit time travel experiment has gone wrong, altering the past and therefore the present, or I have been drawn into a parallel universe as I slept.'
ACTUAL CASE SOLUTION: FBI building had the painters in over the weekend.

X-FILE X-73622
MULDER'S CONCLUSION: 'Assistant Director Skinner did not show up for work today and has seemingly vanished from the face of the earth. I believe that he has either been the victim of an alien abduction or that certain forces within the government have silenced him...
ACTUAL CASE CONCLUSION: Assistant Director Skinner was on a two week vacation.

X-FILE X-74123
MULDER'S CONCLUSION: '...the dead sometimes walk this earth. By what power they do so, we cannot know, but there they are. Walking the streets, stopping in doorways, congregating under streetlights. Terrorising those of us still living. We must bar our doors and pray for daylight once more...'
ACTUAL CASE CONCLUSION: Hallowe'en.

X-FILE X-73388
MULDER'S CONCLUSION: 'Skinner wasn't in his office. All I found was a pile of ash. He had been a victim of spontaneous human combustion...'
ACTUAL CASE CONCLUSION: Skinner had slipped out for a quick sandwich after a morning meeting with the Cigarette Smoking Man.

F.B.I. PERSONNEL FILE

NAME: Fox William Mulder
RANK: Special Agent
BADGE: JTT047101111
CURRENT ASSIGNMENT: Project Head – X-Files

AN INTRODUCTION TO EARTH AND ITS PEOPLE

HEIGHT

The first thing you will notice when you work on Earth is that humans are tall. Very tall. On average, we stand level with a human's crotch. Be thankful that our race's noses have atrophied over the aeons.

Because the humans are tall, they can be very intimidating to those of us not used to them. Resist the temptation to over-compensate, perhaps by wearing stilts during abduction procedures, or investing in expensive and unstylish elevator shoes. Standing on tip-toe fools no one (as does sitting on a fellow Gray's shoulders with a coat over you and referring to yourself as 'Dr Tall from Galaxy Z'). Do not be ashamed to 'walk small'...

SKIN TINCTURE AND EYES

The next thing you will notice is that the humanoids here are not a vibrant and healthy gray like ourselves, but dull tints of pink, brown and orange, which for some reason they refer to as white, black and yellow. It is possible their underdeveloped little eyes perceive the spectrum in a different way to ours.

HAIR

You will also note immediately that humans are unbelievably hairy. As those of you who will work on the breeding programme will soon learn, they even have hair in places you would never imagine. Try not to be afraid.

TEETH

Humans also have teeth and have been known to bite. They are venomous, carrying within their mouths one of the most concentrated toxins yet discovered. If you are bitten, the result can be coma, spasms and almost certain death. They call this substance 'plaque'. Perversely, humans display their teeth when they like you...

DIGITS

Another thing you will quickly notice is that humans have five fingers instead of the normal three. Despite this seeming biological advantage, all that an additional two digits have allowed the human race to achieve is a wider than average repertoire of abusive gestures and a high degree of proficiency in touch typing.

They also have thumbs but – incredibly – have never discovered their true purpose...

GENETIC ENHANCEMENT

Many thousands of years ago, we tried a largely unsuccessful mass genetic alteration programme on the humans, in an attempt to make them more like ourselves. Only vestigial traces of this genetic experiment remain in the human DNA helix, and are only triggered in old age. You will note that the hair drops out, teeth fall out and the individual starts to shrink noticeably...

COMMUNICATION

Humans also employ an extremely eccentric method of communication, unique in the known universe. This is called 'talking'. While they are capable of telepathy – and this is how we communicate with them – they do not normally employ it. Nor do they employ any of the other methods of communication commonly in use, in this galaxy at least. They have no concept of tongue-touching, nose whistles, clucking throat braille, chest-slaps, gastric syncopation, water-flicking or phlegm painting. Even basic penile semaphore is beyond them, although it is believed they use some sort of body language.

FEAR IS YOUR FRIEND

While working with these strange giants on this world of the over-sized, it is natural to be afraid. I am not ashamed to admit to fear. I personally am frightened by basketball players, stilt-walkers and Sigourney Weaver (for more than one reason). Others have expressed fear of overtight trousers, smiling, skyscrapers, tallboys, beehive hairdos, and being made to sit in something called a 'high chair'.

Fear keeps you alert, and will keep you alive. It is your friend.

A BRIEF BUT USEFUL HISTORY OF OPERATIONS

Our work on this planet stretches back some 10,000 standard Earth years. I know. I was one of the very first to arrive here – but my luggage only showed up last Thursday. Our weekly routine was very much the same then as it is now.

Monday	Abduct	Friday	Abduct
Tuesday	Abduct	Saturday	Abduct
Wednesday	Abduct	Sunday	Mutilate cattle
Thursday	Abduct		

The lack of variety has never posed any serious problem to a race with a hive mentality such as ours – although it would have been nice to have had one day off in the last 10,000 years.

Over those years, our great mission has played itself out against the backdrop of human history. Mighty civilisations have risen and fallen. Some have even fallen and then risen. Others rose a bit, fell a bit, rose some more and then went sideways. Some have described a sort of parallelogram. Some went nowhere. Others just fell and fell. Some decided to go and live in the ocean and they all drowned. All have a part to play in our story (except the ones who drowned).

Our hybrid breeding programme has taken many centuries to reach its advanced stage. Many problems had to be overcome, including developing methods which allowed human DNA to bond with ours. For this reason, we have had to abduct millions of humans for medical and breeding purposes. This activity would have been impossible without the active participation of human governments from the very beginning. Because of their unusual appearance (and height), it is extremely difficult for us to work among the humans unobserved. We can sometimes walk among them, wearing human clothes and donning sunglasses to cover our eyes, and thus masquerading as ultra-cool dwarves with advanced male-pattern baldness, but it is far better to have human agents working for us.

As a race, not all humans are immoral, avaricious and greedy – only the ones they appoint as their leaders. This is fortunate for us, as it means human governments may be bribed with 'little gifts' in exchange for allowing us to abduct their citizens.

Today, our operations in America are performed with the active assistance of a powerful group of industrialists, politicians and military figures known as the 'Majestic 12' group. We also have control of large elements of their intelligence bodies including the NSA and CIA and other institutions including NASA and McDonald's (where you will find yourself eligible for a 20% discount).

What do we give them in exchange for their co-operation? Technology mostly. Nothing really important or useful. Nothing too advanced. We simply find out what a civilisation most desires – and give it to them. This we have done since the very earliest days.

For example, when we worked among the 'Beaker People' of Europe some 5,000 years ago, tempting them into dealing with us was simplicity itself, as our records of that time show:

PRIME GRAY: We'd like to abduct more of your people this year. What do you wish in exchange for your co-operation?

LEADER OF BEAKER PEOPLES: Let's see. A beaker, two teacups, a nice chalice, a couple of goblets and a jug...

PRIME GRAY: You drive a hard bargain, great chief, but – very well...

LEADER OF BEAKER PEOPLES: They will have handles, won't they?

PRIME GRAY: Of course. Oh, by the way, do you mind if we shove a rectal probe up your Holy Man?

LEADER OF BEAKER PEOPLES: No, go right ahead. Be my guest. Give us a couple of extra mugs – with handles – and we'll call it all quits...

Some civilisations have been easier to work with than others. We enjoyed an excellent relationship with the Semite people called 'The Philistines' – until fear got the better of us...

All was going well with our 'exchange of merchandise' with the Philistines until one summer's day, on the Plain of Esh-Rabat, I and my assistants met once more in secret with the Philistine leaders in their war tent...

PRIME GRAY: We would wish to increase our harvesting of your people this year, O Philistine Synod. What do you wish in exchange?

MEMBET BEN MEMBET: Have you got any more of those purple bell-bottom trousers? The ones with the green hoops and the chunky one piece belt? They are nicer than our tassled kilts!

GEZER: What about those magic hoops which produce eldritch bubbles when thou dost project thy breath through them?

HORESH: No! I, Bar Horesh of Canaan, do want the canine figurine, the one that does nod when you affix it to the back of thy chariot!

GOLIATH: (Arriving in tent) Hold! Sorry I'm late!

PRIME GRAY: Aghhhh!

GOLIATH: I, Goliath, tallest by far and boldest by nature of all the Philistines do not sell my people for gaudy apparel of the leg nor amusing canine figurines! I want fine drinking vessels emblazoned with the uplifting legend 'World's Best Dad' or headwear that doth appear to be pierced by an arrow... Wait, where are you all going, you gray men of the shortness?

HORESH: Oh, Goliath, your height has scared the little men and the deal is void! Ruin have you brought to Ashkelon and Ashdod, woe have you brought upon the figurine-less, and much shame have you brought upon the clan name of Wul-Worth...

Other civilisations, which initially looked promising, proved to harbour unforeseen difficulties. I will never forget my first – and last – encounter with the people called the Ancient Greeks...

PRIME GRAY: We would have your people for our experiments. What would you have in return?

GREEK SENATOR: Boys!

GREEK CHORUS: Boys! Boys! Boys!

PYTHAGORAS: Er, wisdom, please.

GREEK CHORUS: Oh, shut up Pythagoras! Better to know a milk-skinned cherub of tender years than a fact!

PYTHAGORAS: Fine, don't come crying to me when your triangles don't add up!

GREEK CHORUS: What need have we of the isosceles? What care we for the sum of the square of the hypotenuse! Give us boys, oh diminutive gray!

GREEK SENATOR: Are *you* a boy?

PRIME GRAY: No...

GREEK SENATOR: You look like a boy – short of stature, slender of physique. Big of eye.

PRIME GRAY: Ulp!

GREEK SENATOR: A bald boy, plucked of pate! Come to me boy, and we shall know the Dionysian pleasures of the olive grove!

PRIME GRAY: Eat paralysis ray...!

The Ancient Egyptians were far easier (and safer) to deal with. We tempted their pharaohs with many wonders in exchange for their co-operation (*see over*), but there was one serious drawback... It became increasingly clear to us that the Egyptian civilisation was in decline. Their practice of marrying their own mothers, fathers, sisters, brothers and grandparents was turning them into a race of drooling idiots. Hybrid offspring produced from Egyptian stock had the IQ of string. Some were so retarded, they could not even drool properly. (Hybrids produced in this period were abandoned in a remote region and later became the Turks.)

We turned our attention instead to their slaves, a race called the Israelites then in bondage in Egypt (and quite enjoying it). They had taboos against interbreeding, and consequently enjoyed better genetic stock.

We entered into negotiations for abduction rights with their leader, a man called Moses, who wanted his people freed in exchange for his co-operation. He was not the easiest man to deal with as you will see on page 16...

13

SPECIAL PHARAOHIC EDITION

PAPYRUS
Only 60,000 Abductions.

Head like a sieve? Always forgetting things? Now you can write them down on this handy 'papyrus'. No more carting heavy and cumbersome stone slate tablets on shopping trips! Use this lightweight paper-like substance instead. Great for shopping lists, memos, edicts, doodles, death warrants – you name it, Papyrus does it! Wallpaper your temple! Make Origami figurines! A comfortable and less sore alternative to wiping with bulrushes! You know you want it.

GREAT PYRAMID
Needs assembly.
Only 100,000 Abductions.

MUMMIFICATION
Only 70,000 Abductions.

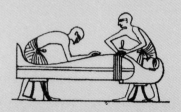

Prepare yourself for the afterlife with this complete mummification kit. Imagine how impressed Anubis will be when you arrive in his kingdom with your brain scraped out through your nose, your vital organs neatly stored away in jars and your body wrapped head to toe in designer bandages and anointed with pungent lotions! Don't leave this life without it! Guaranteed for all eternity. Return for full refund if not accepted into the next world.

▲ It's a solar calculator! ▲ It's a monument! ▲ It's a burial chamber! ▲ It's a razor blade sharpener! ▲ The Great Pyramid is Four things in One! ▲ You'll wonder how you ever managed without one!

Be the first in your Dynasty to own a genuine wonder of the ancient world! Visible for miles! Easy to clean. Lasts for thousands of years – GUARANTEED!

SPHINX

Is it a man? Is it a great cat? Is it a riddle? This ornate garden ornament is sure to liven up any rockery, patio or lawn! Contains 4 x secret chambers handy for garden implements – hoes, rakes, shovels, trowels, mowing chariots etc. Scare off intruders, start spontaneous religious worship, confuse generations to come! No Divine King should be without one.

Only 60,000 Abductions.
Needs assembly. Partially waterproofed.

ABU

Abu here is just two years old and was found wandering lost and lonely in the Mastabas. She's perky, friendly and good with children. Will you give her a home? Show the Goddess Pasht you care!

Only 40,000 Abductions.

PALACE EUNUCHS

Beautifully castrated young males. Ideal for guarding your harem and talking in funny high pitched voices.

An ideal topic of dinner conversation, and a great butt of cruel cheap jokes when things aren't going too well and you need to raise a laugh.

A 'snip' at only... 30,000 Abductions.

YOUR SISTER

Go on, you know you want to! Make her your wife, your concubine. Keep power in the family, where it belongs! Plus – no strange in-laws, guaranteed, because her parents are your parents (and also probably your aunts and uncles, your great nephews, your own grandparents, their own grandparents, your sons and daughters and close friends of the family). It's hard to keep track, you incestuous little devils!

Only 30,000 Abductions.

MOSES: Frogs?

PRIME GRAY: Yes.

MOSES: Frogs. Aaron and I are supposed to go to Pharaoh and threaten him with frogs?

PRIME GRAY: Yes.

MOSES: *Excuse me, Mr Pharaoh, but if you don't let the Israelites leave Egypt, my God says he's going to 'smite thy borders with a plague of frogs'. Better watch out, Ramses, because a big frog might land on your head?*

AARON: Oooh, scary...

PRIME GRAY: A lot of people don't like frogs...

MOSES: What about, *if you don't let my people go, my God's going to blow your family jewels off!*

AARON: Oh yes, that's a lot better.

PRIME GRAY: I can do toads. They're bigger, and they can give you warts...

MOSES: What about, *let my people go or I'll kill you, you fucker?* That's straightforward enough.

PRIME GRAY: Newts, now there's an attractive idea you must admit...

MOSES: No frogs, no newts, no toads, no salamanders, no chameleons, no iguanas, no monitor lizards – no amphibians of any kind.

PRIME GRAY: Cheese...

MOSES: A plague of *cheese?*

AARON: What kind?

MOSES: Shut up, you putz! All right, frogs are fine – but big frogs. Friggin' big, huge, enormous frogs. With fangs. Frogs trained to kill. Killer frogs. Frogs of war.

PRIME GRAY: I'll see what I can do...

Eventually, we freed the Israelites, and they followed one of our ships out of Egypt and into Canaan. Despite the fact that one of our scout ships was always there, by day and by night, to guide them, Moses' stubborn insistence on doing more and more himself got his people into trouble.

PRIME GRAY: You've been wandering in the wilderness for forty years now, Moses. Let us help you.

MOSES: I don't need your help. I can do it.

PRIME GRAY: The map's the wrong way up, Moses.

MOSES: I know, I know... Go away.

PRIME GRAY: We can help you, Moses.

MOSES: I don't need your help. I haven't forgiven you for those frogs yet. They were bloody useless. I felt such an idiot. *Let my people go, Ribbit! Ribbit!*

PRIME GRAY: It was bad for us too, Moses. Many of the frogs escaped from our breeding vats and have infested our ships. Periodically we must flush them out of the airlocks and they cause much confusion among the humans as they rain down...

MOSES: And now you're teaching my people bad habits. They've seen you abducting their cattle at night – or, at least they've seen the cattle flying into the air. Now they're worshipping a golden calf!

PRIME GRAY: Sorry about that, we made that mistake with the Hindus! Look, if we help you sort out a more sensible religion, are we friends again?

MOSES: Possibly...

PRIME GRAY: We shall give you five holy commandments to live by.

MOSES: Twelve.

PRIME GRAY: Seven.

MOSES: Ten.

PRIME GRAY: Done!

From these early examples of our work in collaborating with the humans, I am sure you will begin to grasp the complexities of our relationship with them. With the advent of mass media – when total exposure may be no further away than 'film at 11' – today more than ever it is important to keep what we do a closely guarded secret.

Which brings us back to the X-Files and attempts by humans hostile to our plans to expose us. Study well how we have dealt with this problem – and be prepared...

UFO SECRETS OF
THE THIRD REICH

Throughout history, we have been forced to deal with some of the most wretched specimens of humanity – Attila the Hun, Ivan the Terrible, Louis the Bastard, Genghis Khan, the Borgia Popes, Torquemada, Caligula, Nero, Napoleon and Woodrow Wilson.

So we had no qualms in approaching the emerging Nazi dictator, Adolf Hitler, to propose a deal. In fact, he had much to recommend him. He was short, didn't smile very often and had an unusually advanced interest in genetic engineering – as he had long believed himself to be a woman trapped in a man's body...

I and one of my most trusted assistants made the initial contact in his private chambers late one night in 1942.

HITLER: Ah...Ah...Ah...Ah...Eurgh...Eurgh...Ah...Ah...

PRIME GRAY: I knew this was going to happen. We materialise
in someone's bedroom late at night unannounced – it's inevitable.

ASSISTANT: Are we in the right room? I though Hitler was German
but he looks Japanese.

HITLER: Who are you? Get out! Get out!

PRIME GRAY: Hang on a minute, Hitler. I've told them time and again.
Monitor the room before you send us in...

ASSISTANT: Where is his love partner? I cannot see one.

HITLER: Guards! Guards!

PRIME GRAY: They're paralysed, just like you. Would you like us to
come back when you've finished?

HITLER: Why? I was not doing anything...

PRIME GRAY: We come from...

HITLER: ...my wardrobe – yes I know.

ASSISTANT: No...

PRIME GRAY: Yes...Yes, that's right. We come from your wardrobe, Herr Hitler. So we are the...the...

HITLER: You're the little goblin men...

PRIME GRAY: ...who live in your wardrobe – of course we are (oh no! It's George III all over again).

HITLER: Yes, you live between my jackboots and my copies of *Nazi Naturist*. I used to tell Goering and Bormann all about you but I think they didn't believe me. But I knew you were there. I used to hear you playing soccer at night, kicking a mothball from one side of the wardrobe to the other...

PRIME GRAY: We want you to...

HITLER: And sometimes you spoke to me. '*Adolf, Adolf,*' you would say, '*Invade Russia in winter,*' or '*Take on the Royal Air Force over England.*' That's how I stay one step ahead of the cursed Allied forces!

PRIME GRAY: And we'll continue to help you win the war if you...

HITLER: Which one of you is Bongo and which one is Ippy? Ah. It is so good to see you after so many years! You are taller than I imagined.

ASSISTANT: Thank you. So are you.

HITLER: I am overjoyed that you are here. Did you like the marzipan I used to leave in the wardrobe for you? I have a million and one questions, like where did you go to the toilet? Did you tangle all my coat hangers? But now, enough. Tomorrow I will hold a vast rally at Nuremberg and announce that we cannot lose this war because the wardrobe goblin men are here!

PRIME GRAY: No, no. This must be our little secret. We've got to go now, back to our...our...

HITLER: Furniture wonderland.

PRIME GRAY: That's it, Mein Fuhrer. That's right. We'll see you soon.

HITLER: Mein Gott! They have vanished. I can move again.
Ah...Ah...Ah...Ah...Ahhhhhhhhhhhhhhhhhhhhhhhhhhhhhhhh!

Despite this rather unpromising start, we did manage to establish a good working relationship with the Third Reich.

Their scientists were only too eager to talk to us. Guided by his invisible friends, Hitler had already ordered the building of a vast array of 'terror weapons' of his very own devising. However, there was some degree of scepticism among the German high command and scientific establishment that these weapons would play any real part in the war effort:

THE V-1: A ROCKET-PROPELLED PIG NAMED FRITZ

THE V-2: GROUND-TO-AIR LIVERWURST

THE V-3: BLITZKRIEG POGO-STICKS FOR A SURPRISE ATTACK

THE V-4: A FLANNAGAN AND ALLEN SEEKING MISSILE

THE V-5: A DEVICE THAT WOULD PROJECT AN IMAGE OF AN ORANGE, A BAR OF CHOCOLATE AND SOME NYLON STOCKINGS ON TO CLOUDS OVER LONDON, REMINDING THEM OF THE RATIONING THEY HAD TO ENDURE AND THEREFORE BREAKING THEIR SPIRIT

THE V-6: A PLAGUE OF LOCUSTS, EACH ONE WITH A STICK GRENADE TIED TO ITS BACK LEGS, LAUNCHED BY STEAM CATAPULT AS THEY WERE TOO HEAVY TO FLY

THE V-7: A GENETICALLY MUTATED PRAYING MANTIS 300 FEET HIGH. CALLED BORIS.

THE V-8: A LONG-RANGE BOMBER MADE ENTIRELY OF BLACK FOREST GATEAU THAT TASTED EVERY BIT AS GOOD AS IT HANDLED, AND SO WOULD PROVIDE THE CREW WITH SUSTENANCE IF THEY WERE SHOT DOWN IN A REMOTE LOCATION...

THE V-9: A GLIDER-TOWED TANK

THE V-10: A TANK-TOWED GLIDER

THE V-11: THE 1x1x1 (A RADICAL NEW BOMBER THAT COULD CARRY ONE POUND OF BOMBS ONE MILE AT A SPEED OF ONE MILE AN HOUR – AND COULD ONLY BE USED ONCE)

THE V-12: THE 2x2x2 (AN IMPROVED VERSION OF THE V-11)

THE V-13: A BOMB WHICH CHANGES THE SEX OF EVERYONE IN A 12 MILE BLAST RADIUS, THUS TURNING THE ADVANCING 4TH ARMY INTO A BUNCH OF RATHER FETCHING YOUNG WOMEN. (DESPITE REPEATED REQUESTS BY THE FUHRER FOR THIS BOMB TO BE TESTED ON BERLIN ITSELF, THE WAR ENDED BEFORE IT COULD BE USED)

In return for the rights to carry out our own genetic programme, we aided the Nazi's V-weapons campaign, teaching their scientists how to build rockets. We exchanged genetic information too. The Nazis were highly advanced in this area and we learned much from them before the war finally ended and the scientists fled to America.

Fifty years later, little did we guess that our past associations would be coming back to haunt us...

**TRANSCRIPT OF NSA PHONE TAPPING OPERATION ON RESIDENCE OF
MRS MULDER, 2790 VINE STREET, CHILMARK, MASSACHUSETTS.**

RING RING

MRS MULDER: Hello?

VOICE: What is Samantha Mulder's middle name?

MRS MULDER: Anne...

VOICE: And what did you give to Fox for his eighth birthday?

MRS MULDER: A Major Matt Mason space doll.

VOICE: It was NOT a doll, Ma! It was an action figure! OK, what did you used to say to Fox as a baby?

MRS MULDER: Don't play with that: it'll fall off.

VOICE: No...apart from that, Ma...

MRS MULDER: How's my little Foxy-Woxy?

VOICE: OK, it's you. Hello, Ma.

MRS MULDER: Hello Fox. Do we have to go through with this every time you call?

VOICE *(now positively identified as Agent Mulder):* I've had my fill of alien shape changers, Ma...

MRS MULDER: Yes, I'm sure you have dear...

AGENT MULDER: Your own best friend could be one and you'd never know...

MRS MULDER: Mrs Silverman? Oh no, I don't think so dear. If she could change shape, she wouldn't be so...plump. Anyway it's very nice to hear from you. And how's that lovely girl, Dana? Fox, you could do a lot worse...and you're not getting any younger.

AGENT MULDER: Listen Ma, don't say anything too much...because there might be a bug on the line, but you remember that thing Dad used to do at the State Department?

MRS MULDER: Fox! I don't think we should talk about that now. The poor man's dead. He couldn't help it. He was under such pressure at work. It never went on his record. How did you find out about it?

AGENT MULDER: Er...No ma, I meant his job. Did he ever leave any...papers with you after you split up...State papers? Journals?

FLAG: MJ-12 RED ALERT. IMMEDIATE NOTIFICATION. RE: MERCHANDISE/ORG/FATHERLAND/'GERMAN SHEPHERD'/NJB

MRS MULDER: There might be some of his things left in the attic...

AGENT MULDER: I'll come straight round...

MRS MULDER: You only visit when you want something. It was my birthday yest...

-CLICK-

By the time I reached my mother's house, *they* had beaten me to it. The house was a smoking ruin. I rushed from my car in a total panic. Had the documents survived? As I started digging in the rubble with my bare hands trying to find a journal, a file, anything – I was interrupted by my mother, who had no idea what had just happened. She told me that she had never had one of her recipes explode before in forty years. I tried to explain that the government had attempted to kill her, but she wouldn't have any of it. 'They wouldn't try and kill me – I voted for them,' she told me. Any further argument was useless, so I left her to be stretchered away to the burns unit while I concentrated on finding whatever still remained of my father's papers.

I found just one solitary singed scrap – but what a scrap. It read, in my father's own handwriting,

> 10.30am Meeting with Adolf Hitler, who is alive & well and living in Hollywood as the movie sta
>
> 3pm Collect dry cleaning

It was incredible! Hitler had survived the war and been given a new identity – or more likely, switched identities with a movie star of the time. He hadn't travelled on board a U-Boat to Atlantis, after all!

To avoid suspicion he must have looked exactly like the star he replaced – but Hitler was easily identifiable by his very distinctive moustache. Then it dawned on me! Who, in Hollywood bore an exact likeness to Hitler – down to his moustache? None other than the great *Charlie Chaplin*!

That meant that it was the Little Tramp who had been found dead in the Bunker that fateful day in April 1945 – while Hitler had taken his place up on the silver screen. No wonder he never made another decent movie again after the war.

I thought about it deep into the night. The physical similarities between the two men were uncanny. Perhaps too uncanny. About five in the morning I began to wonder – perhaps they were clones. I looked deeper and found some amazing coincidences between their supposedly separate lives:

Hitler & Chaplin: Clones or coincidence?

	Adolf Hitler	Charlie Chaplin
Date of birth:	April 1889	April 1889
Artistic leanings:	Yes: painter	Yes: child performer
Nickname:	Yes: die Fuhrer	Yes: the Little Tramp (Hitler was also a tramp after WW1)
Facial hair:	Yes: small moustache	Yes: small moustache
Props:	Yes: funny hat and baggy trousers	Yes: funny hat and baggy trousers
Funny walk:	Yes: goosestep	Yes: bow-legged waddle
Girlfriend:	Yes: Eva Braun	Yes: Mary Pickford
Liked throwing things:	Yes: tantrums	Yes: custard pies
Wrote autobiography:	Yes: *Mein Kampf*	Yes: *My Life In Movies*
Significant event in 1919	Yes: joined German Workers Party	Yes: joined United Artists
Significant event in 1940	Yes: Europe's leading dictator	Yes: starred in *The Great Dictator*
Accompanied by small being:	Yes: Heinrich Himmler	Yes: Jackie Coogan
Loved by millions of adoring fans	Yes	Yes
Genius:	Yes (evil one)	Yes (comic one)

The proof is irrefutable, I believe, and this has led me to investigate whether other Nazi leaders were secretly given asylum in the US, by posing as silent comedians. The physical similarities are too close to be purely coincidental:

Goebbels and Goering = Laurel and Hardy
Heinrich Himmler = Harold Lloyd
Rudolph Hess = Buster Keaton
Leading members of the
Gestapo = The Keystone Kops

A routine check of Mulder's computer files revealed that – while he had stumbled on to something extremely significant – he had, as usual, completely misinterpreted it.

By the beginning of 1945, the Nazis knew the war was lost. Fearing the Russians, they started to plan for a new life – in America. The rocket scientists were embraced with open arms by the US-sponsored Operation Paperclip, but more mundane Nazis were not so welcome...

Combining our genetic knowledge with that already developed by the Nazis themselves, we helped to forge new identities for the fleeing Nazis, so that they could be smuggled into America, aided and abetted by sympathisers from the American Office of Strategic Services, or OSS...

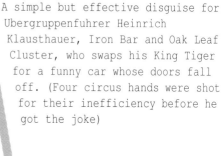

A simple but effective disguise for Ubergruppenfuhrer Heinrich Klausthauer, Iron Bar and Oak Leaf Cluster, who swaps his King Tiger for a funny car whose doors fall off. (Four circus hands were shot for their inefficiency before he got the joke)

Field Marshall Wilhelm 'The Butcher of Bremen' Mueller prepares to follow a new sort of orders...

Hitler bids farewell to a
genetically transformed
Martin Bormann on his
(failed) mission to become
another Shirley Temple.

Nazi scientists' attempts to
create authentic negroid features
fail, condemning several elite
members of the Gestapo to a life
as middle-of-the road vaudeville
entertainers...

Air ace Luft Major Willy von
Brandt uses all his skill to
land on a turd.

Kurt Waldheim sets off to be
Secretary General of the
United Nations.

THE WHITE HOUSE
WASHINGTON

PRESIDENTIAL BRIEFING FOR PRESIDENT HARRY S TRUMAN
MONDAY 5th NOVEMBER 1945

TOP SECRET

**TOP SECRET / MAJIC
EYES ONLY**

IN ATTENDANCE
President Harry S Truman
Mr Allen Dulles, OSS and guest
Mr William Mulder, State Department
OSS Secretary N J Baker
OSS Secretary M J Kopechne

****
CLASSIFIED
****
LEVEL 16 [AND ABOVE]

DOCUMENT **001**

MINUTES

PRESIDENT TRUMAN: Nazis! Nazis! Nazis!
Nazis everywhere! Did you smuggle in the
whole of blasted Nazi Germany, you little
weasel? I told you after the rocket
scientists - no more Nazis. And what do I
get...more Nazis. I am surrounded by
Nazis! And who's this 'special advisor'
you brought with you, Allen..?

ALLEN DULLES: Reinhard Gehlen...

PRESIDENT TRUMAN: Sure sounds like a
Nazi...Is he a Nazi?

ALLEN DULLES: Nazi-ish...

PRESIDENT TRUMAN: Out! Get out!

ALLEN DULLES: Wait, Mr President. He's got
something incredible to show you...
something that wants to meet you...

MR GEHLEN LEAVES THE ROOM AND RETURNS
SHORTLY THEREAFTER WITH AN
EXTRATERRESTRIAL BIOLOGICAL ENTITY

COLONEL GEHLEN: Herr President, Ladies and
Gentlemen, may I present a being from
another world...

[FOUR HOURS LATER]
PRESIDENT TRUMAN: He's what?

ALLEN DULLES: An alien.

[TWO HOURS LATER]
PRESIDENT TRUMAN: Run this by me again. He
wants to do a deal with us. We get all his
advanced alien technology and in return...

WILLIAM MULDER: He gets...to abduct and
experiment on American citizens.

PRIME GRAY: Who will be returned unharmed
afterwards, Mr Mulder. A fair deal, I
believe, for superior technology such as
this...

PRESIDENT TRUMAN: What in tarnation is
that?

PRIME GRAY: We call it - a 'Post-It
Note'...

PRESIDENT TRUMAN: Gee, now that could be
useful. The lab boys will want to examine
that. Hey, Dulles, I bet the Commies
haven't got one of these...

PRIME GRAY: That's just the start of what
we can give you, Mr President, in
exchange for your co-operation.

PRESIDENT TRUMAN: You got more gadgets
like this?

PRIME GRAY: This is a highly advanced
version of what you call 'a pen'. You see,
this way up the bathing beauty is demurely
dressed, but turn the pen up this way -
and the girl is magically naked....

PRESIDENT TRUMAN: Wow! Her swimsuit's vanished! Hubba, hubba! Hey Allen, check this out! Wowee! Now you see it, now you don't! Now you see it, now you don't!

PRIME GRAY: I'm glad you like it, Mr President...

PRESIDENT TRUMAN: Now you see it, now you don't! That is hot!

WILLIAM MULDER: Very good, but what about safe nuclear energy? We have tried to harness...

PRIME GRAY: All in good time, sir. We will open all our technological advances to you in time. Take this, for example...

PRESIDENT TRUMAN: It's a spring! Wow! That's fantastic!

WILLIAM MULDER: We've already got that, sir. We already have spring technology.

PRIME GRAY: But this is no ordinary spring, Mr Mulder. That's why we call it...the Slinky...

PRESIDENT TRUMAN: What does it do? What does it do?

PRIME GRAY: Where are your nearest stairs?

[MEETING ADJOURNED FOR FOUR HOURS]

PRESIDENT TRUMAN: That's the darndest thing I ever saw! Does it use anti-gravity?

WILLIAM MULDER: No sir, it works precisely because of gravity.

PRESIDENT TRUMAN: I was close. I gotta have another go...

PRIME GRAY: So we have an agreement?

PRESIDENT TRUMAN: Yeah! Where do I sign? Can I use that pen with the swimsuit?

WILLIAM MULDER: I think the President would like time to think about it...

PRIME GRAY: Very well. I shall return tomorrow.

EXTRATERRESTRIAL BIOLOGICAL ENTITY VANISHES

PRESIDENT TRUMAN: Where'd he go?

WILLIAM MULDER: What's your part in all this, Dulles? What do you want for fixing this up?

ALLEN DULLES: I just want to keep the OSS going with one small change. We drop the 'O'...

WILLIAM MULDER: You want to set up the SS in America?

PRESIDENT TRUMAN: They're Nazis, aren't they?

ALLEN DULLES: We won't call it the SS. How does 'The Central Intelligence Agency' grab you?

COLONEL GEHLEN: Can I join?

ALLEN DULLES: You're in.

PRESIDENT TRUMAN: Nazis, Nazis everywhere. I'm only surprised Adolf godamn Hitler himself isn't here...

MISS BAKER, MR ALLEN DULLES' SECRETARY, ENTERS WITH COFFEE

COLONEL GEHLEN: Heil Hitler!

ALLEN DULLES: Heil Hitler!

MISS BAKER: Heil, mein kammarraden.

ALLEN DULLES: Mr President, perhaps you should meet my new secretary, Miss Norma Jean Baker...

THE ROSWELL INCIDENT & MAJESTIC-12

TRANSCRIPT OF NSA PHONE TAPPING OPERATION ON RESIDENCE OF FBI SPECIAL AGENT FOX MULDER, APARTMENT 42, 3412 WEST ST. ALEXANDRIA VA

AGENT MULDER: Scully, sorry to disturb you at home, but you got to come over. There's this video you've just got to see...

AGENT SCULLY: Mulder, I haven't the slightest interest in watching any tape you have...

AGENT MULDER: It's business, not pleasure Scully. I've got the Roswell autopsy tape...the real one.

FLAG: MJ-12 RED ALERT. IMMEDIATE NOTIFICATION. RE: MERCHANDISE/ROSWELL/AREA 51

AGENT SCULLY: Since when was Traci Lords at Roswell, Mulder?

AGENT MULDER: Scully, this is the real thing. X dropped it off tonight, along with a bag of – get this Scully – actual metal fragments from the crash. We'll watch it together. Come on over...and bring the popcorn...

Fifty years on, the Roswell Incident still marks a low point in our relations with the American government. We had been so careful not to let anything worthwhile fall into their hands...and suddenly they had a crashed craft in their possession...

Following the crash, the humans denied any knowledge of the incident...

They had not retrieved our downed craft. There was nothing in Hangar 18. They hadn't cut one of us up and put him in several thousand separate petri dishes. They hadn't captured one of us alive and stuck him in a glass case and played him Mozart and Verdi until he puked. They weren't trying to spawn their own hybrids from scraps of our DNA and they certainly weren't trying to retro engineer our spacecraft technology at any secret base in Nevada.

Despite their protestations, we had strong reason to believe they were lying to us...

USAAF

TOP SECRET / MAJIC
EYES ONLY

TOP SECRET

DATE   2 JULY 1947   TIME 23.50hrs

SOURCE AND EVALUATION: General Roger Ramey, Carswell AAFB, TX

SUMMARY OF INFORMATION

Unconfirmed Mayday message received as follows

TRANSMISSION: Mayday, Mayday. Can anyone hear me, over?

ROSWELL TOWER: This is Roswell Field calling unidentified air traffic... Reading you 5 by 5. State your call sign. Over.

TRANSMISSION: Roswell Field, this is Glenn Miller in a Flying Saucer, over...

ROSWELL TOWER: Unidentified air traffic...where have you been for the last three years?

TRANSMISSION: Don't ask. Over...

ROSWELL TOWER: Unidentified air traffic...uhhh...what is the nature of your Mayday? Over.

TRANSMISSION: Roswell Field, I'm bent double in a four foot high cupola dome with three unconscious alien beings and I don't know how to fly this thing. Over...

ROSWELL TOWER: Uh...Roger that. Standby...Uh, we don't believe a word of this down here. Over.

TRANSMISSION: SOUND OF TROMBONE PLAYING 'IN THE MOOD'.

ROSWELL TOWER: Welcome home, Colonel Miller, sir! Stay calm, sir, I've got USAAF's most experienced pilot here beside me. He'll talk you down. I'm handing over to him now...*Hello, Colonel Miller, this is Wing Commander Bradley. Can you play 'Little Brown Jug'? Over.*

TRANSMISSION: Get me down, I'm losing altitude. Over!

ROSWELL TOWER: OK. Can you see the horizon? Over.

TRANSMISSION: No...there's no windows. Over.

ROSWELL TOWER: Tell me your instrument readings. Over.

TRANSMISSION: There are no instruments. Over...

ROSWELL TOWER: OK...um...I want you to pull back gently on the throttle... Over.

TRANSMISSION: There is no throttle - just twenty glowing hemispheres that change colour when I touch them. Over...

ROSWELL TOWER: Er...standby....Er...press them all. Over.

TRANSMISSION: Are you sure? Over.

ROSWELL TOWER: Well, it couldn't do you any harm. Over ...hello, Unidentified air traffic...unidentified air traffic, do you read? Do you read? Over.

Date forwarded HQ AFOSI 3 July 1947
AFOSI FORM AS ATTACHED [ ] Yes [ ] No

Roger Ramey.

MAJOR JESSE MARCEL, STAFF INTELLIGENCE OFFICER AT THE 509TH BOMB
GROUP INTELLIGENCE OFFICE DISPLAYS MYSTERIOUS DEBRIS...

The possibility that Agent Mulder now had genuine evidence of Roswell in his possession was too good an opportunity to miss. One of our leading Special Operations Experts was sent down to retrieve the cassette, and replace it with an exquisitely crafted forgery...

REPORT TO PRIME GRAY FROM SPECIAL OPERATIONS

<u>Attempt 1</u>: Cunningly disguised as Bigfoot I stood outside Agent Mulder's apartment and threw stones up at the window. After some fifteen minutes he took notice and gave pursuit. I doubled back, abandoned my costume and made my way up to his apartment. Unfortunately he had locked the door behind him – an eventuality I had not anticipated.
<u>Attempt 2</u>: Tried to gain entry by climbing in air conditioning ducts. Got in feet first but misjudged dimensions and got head firmly wedged in duct. Emergency recovery team dispatched to rescue me but subsequently become firmly wedged as well. Panic ensues. Mother ship dispatched to mid-West, abducts cow to produce butter for use as a lubricant. Further recovery team appeared with freshly made butter and liberated us.
<u>Attempt 3</u>: Went up to Agent Mulder's front door. Knocked on door and hid to one side. When Mulder opened the door, crawled between his legs and scurried behind sofa. While Agent Mulder was in the bathroom, grabbed tape from VCR, replaced it with hoax tape. Found evidence bag and swapped it over. Tried to let myself out. Panic ensued when I discovered I could not reach door handle. Drawing on my extensive covert operations training I curled up in a foetal position behind his sofa and moaned. Fortunately the doorbell rang. Agent Scully had arrived. Took the opportunity to crawl between both their legs into corridor and escaped with tape and evidence.

Despite the Roswell Incident, we maintained contact with the humans who were very keen to continue a dialogue and whose craving for our technology was driven by President Truman and his desire to stay one step ahead of the Russians – especially in the area of 'Advanced Spring Technology'.

However, Mr William Mulder of the US State Department kept pressing us to supply the secrets of safe atomic energy – and we kept delaying him – or changing the subject altogether.

Eventually we knew we couldn't delay things any longer and decided to come clean about safe atomic power...

PRESIDENTIAL BRIEFING FOR PRESIDENT HARRY S TRUMAN
MONDAY 8 SEPTEMBER 1947

DOCUMENT 007

TRANSCRIPT OF MEETING

PRESIDENT TRUMAN: What do you mean 'it doesn't exist'?

PRIME GRAY: That's right, sir.

PRESIDENT TRUMAN: Well, that's a shame...

WILLIAM MULDER: So you're saying that there's no way we can harness safe atomic energy?

GEN. ROBERT MONTAGUE: My God! All our work at the Atomic Energy Commission has been in vain. This must never get out! Everyone in this room will have to be shot...

ALLEN DULLES: I can take care of that...

PRIME GRAY: I am sorry General, but I think it is only fair that you know the truth.

PRESIDENT TRUMAN: But I thought you guys were so advanced that you must know how to handle it.

PRIME GRAY: Mr President, there are three forces in the universe that are beyond control. One of these is Fghhyteju, one is Xgdx and the other is what you call atomic energy. It is intrinsically uncontrollable and the radiation it produces kills - no matter how tall you are.

ALLEN DULLES: What's this Fghhyteju stuff? Can we have it? How dangerous is it? Could it reach Moscow?

GEN. ROBERT MONTAGUE: Can we build reactors for it? Is it cheaper than nuclear energy?

WILLIAM MULDER: So we'll never be able to harness atomic energy?

PRESIDENT TRUMAN: So there's no way that we'll have atomic Studebakers?

PRIME GRAY: No.

PRESIDENT TRUMAN: Or washing machines powered by uranium?

PRIME GRAY: I'm afraid not.

PRESIDENT TRUMAN: You mean to say that no American family will ever be self-sufficient, thanks to their own atomic pile the size of a cereal box?

PRIME GRAY: I have to regretfully say no, again, Sir.

PRESIDENT TRUMAN: OK then, my little friends. What *can* you give me?

WILLIAM MULDER: Sir, with respect I think we should question the EBE on atomic energy more fully...

GEN. ROBERT MONTAGUE: I agree. We've invested millions of dollars and man hours at Sandia Base. We must press for more information...

PRESIDENT TRUMAN: Gentlemen, if our short, bald friend here says it's impossible, then it's impossible...

WILLIAM MULDER: But Sir, atomic energy is the key...

PRESIDENT TRUMAN: Bill. Look, I like you but I'm in charge. Let's forget about this whole atomic energy doo-dad and see what other great things the alien can give us. Remember that Slinky device? Goddamn marvel if ever I've seen one. And what about that little bird that keeps bobbing his head into a glass of whiskey? Bet the goddamn Russkies don't have that baby in their arsenal!

PRIME GRAY: Mr President, are you interested in automobiles?

PRESIDENT TRUMAN: Sure am, ol' gray buddy.

WILLIAM MULDER: Sir, I really do think that...

PRESIDENT TRUMAN: Shut it Bill. Tell me about the cars, boy.

PRIME GRAY: Well, in lieu of atomic energy, and for cooperating with us, we will give you the technological secrets of the wraparound windshield, automatic transmission and two-tone paintwork. These holographic projections will show their potential.

PRESIDENT TRUMAN: Two-tone paint? That's incredible. Do you see that Bill? Green and Mauve - on one car? On one car!

WILLIAM MULDER: Sir, please, if I can...

PRIME GRAY: May I also present the powered hardtop?

PRESIDENT TRUMAN: My God! Just one press of a button and the whole goddamn roof disappears. Now you see it - now you don't! Now you see it - now you don't! Wowee! Those Commie bastards are gonna be real sore!

PRIME GRAY: And finally...tail fins.

PRESIDENT TRUMAN: Tail fins! Tail fins! Incredible. (SINGS) My eyes have seen the glory of the coming of the Lord! General Montague. See those. *That's* what you should be spending money on! Bill, this is marvellous. It's the eighth wonder of the goddamn world! Those chrome trims and torpedo lights! I think I've died and gone to Detroit heaven. OK Gray man. Gimme those beauts and you can have anything you damn well want. Abduct General Montague here and now if you like.

GEN. ROBERT MONTAGUE: Sir!

PRESIDENT TRUMAN: Go on...probe the bastard!

Over all protests from his advisors, President Truman pressed for an official business contract to be drawn up, as is the American way.

He also established a special committee to oversee the negotiations and handle the 'merchandise' (see page 36-7) they would receive from us.

This committee was known as 'Majestic 12'.

TOP SECRET / MAJIC
EYES ONLY

Warning: This is a TOP SECRET - EYES ONLY document containing compartmentalised information essential to the national security of the United States. EYES ONLY ACCESS to the material herein is strictly limited to those possessing Majestic-12 clearance level. Reproduction in any form or the taking of written or mechanically transcribed notes is strictly forbidden.

Note: OPERATION MAJESTIC-12 is a TOP SECRET Research and Development/Intelligence operation responsible only to the President of the United States. Operations of the project are carried out under control of the Majestic-12 (Majic-12) Group which was established by special classified executive order of President Truman on 24 September 1947, upon recommendation by Dr. Vannevar Bush and Secretary James Forrestal.

Subject: Contract between the United States government (hereafter known as the 'US') and Extraterrestrial Biological Entities (hereafter known as 'EBEs').

Clause 1:
Mutual respect between parties should be observed at all times. The US promises not to refer to EBEs, whether in their company or not, by the following terms: shorty, squirt, runt-features, dustbutt, titch, knee-high, half-pint, peewee, Gray Geeks, or 'here come the dickless'.

Clause 2:
In a reciprocal display of respect, the EBEs promise to avert their gaze from humans' groins when they talk to them, as humans find this unnerving.

Clause 3:
The US shall give unlimited freedom to EBEs to use its airspace, land their craft and abduct humans and/or animals as deemed necessary for genetic experimentation.

Clause 4:
The US shall let the EBEs go about their business without hindrance from local, federal or military forces providing Clauses 5 to 16 are met (especially Clause 5).

Clause 5:
For the purpose of this contract, genetic experiments are interpreted to mean the creation of a human/EBE hybrid and not cloning Jerry Lewis. This point is not negotiable.

Clause 6:
Human abductions on US territories shall be limited to 500,000 per annum without prior written consent from the President.

Clause 7:
The US shall cover up any reports of alien craft by issuing credible scientific explanations for these sightings, including stray weather balloons, temperature inversions, lenticular cloud formations, meteors, swamp gas, the planet Venus or city lights reflecting off the bellies of low-flying Canadian geese.

Clause 8:
The US shall cover up any reports of human abductions by issuing credible scientific explanations for these claims including sleep walking, alcoholic delusions, being 'one sandwich short of a picnic' or pure bullshit.

Clause 9:
In return for the above mentioned opportunities, the EBEs shall make available technology to the US which up until now has been beyond its scientific capabilities, especially in the areas of automobile design and advanced spring technology.

Clause 10:
If the EBEs do figure out a way to use atomic power safely then the US shall be the first to benefit (particularly if it results in atomic powered cars, or springs).

Clause 11:
Such technology shall be offered on an exclusive basis to the US and not one hint of an advanced idea or theory should be shared with the Eastern Bloc.

Clause 12:
The US Government agrees to conceal the EBEs' previous involvement with the Nazi regime in Germany.

Clause 13:
This contract is legally binding under US law although we admit that we're not sure how it stands up under extra-terrestrial jurisdiction.

Clause 14:
The EBEs will, within one Earth calendar month, prepare a document outlining the technology they propose to let us have in exchange for abduction rights.

Clause 15:
The contract can be terminated by either party in writing. However a notice period of one Earth calendar year must be given. Verbal or telepathic notice is not acceptable. Time dilation may not be used to shorten or lengthen said notice period.

Clause 16:
Should any disputes arise during the activities outlined in this agreement, these will be settled by negotiation and not destruction of people, property or land masses by molecular decomposition, heat ray, Z-Gun or any other advanced weaponry which we don't have (yet).

MERCHANDISE CATALOGUE

Where People Mean Points – and Points Mean Prizes!

The Frisbee

Designed on genuine 'Flying Saucer' principles, the Frisbee can be used either to create hoax UFO photographs to discredit witnesses, or as a toy for children and medium-to-large sized dogs. A godsend for picnics! Turned upside down, it instantly becomes a food dish!

ONLY 50,000 ABDUCTIONS

Does not require batteries
Colour may differ from that shown.

TV DINNERS

Here's a time saving 'must have' for the civilisation that's really going places! A ready to serve three-course meal in just minutes instead of hours. Each 'plastipack blister', contains meat derivative, strangely symmetrical potatoes and disconcertingly bright vegetables splashed with flecks of dessert. Blistering heat in the centre and refreshing coolness on the outside makes each mealtime a feast of discovery!

ONLY 80,000 ABDUCTIONS

MICROWAVE REQUIRED.
Colour may vary from that normally associated with these food products

Smallpox Vaccination

Eliminate a major disease and implant whatever else you like at the same time. Keep people dull and stupid, make them carnally responsive to ageing industrialists, make them grow three legs – the fun's just starting when you choose 'Smallpox Vaccination'. Get invaluable genetic data on your population, inoculate foreigners and reduce their IQ by up to 60%, etc. Sterilise, kill, control – what more could you want?

ONLY 100,000 ABDUCTIONS

Batteries not required

Superball

Utilising top secret alien polymer technology and computer-designed kinetic energy enhancement algorithms, this handy dandy little ball bounces as high as a house! Every major civilisation should have one.

ONLY 150,000 ABDUCTIONS

No batteries required
Choice of day-glo colours

PLASTIC

The wonder material of the future! You'll wonder how you ever managed without it! Ideal for making cheap and mildly toxic toys, disposable cutlery, records, drinking cups, novelty masks, etc.

ONLY 400,000 ABDUCTIONS

Requires assembly.

ORGAN TRANSPLANTS

Do your voters consider you heartless? Get a new one – or a liver, or a kidney! It's simple with 'organ transplant'!

We'll teach you all you need to know, including how it's done, and how to make sure only rich people stand a chance of getting a new donor organ! Now, even the lowest of Southern White Trash can be put to good use. Add years to your life! End theirs prematurely! Includes instruction manual and starter organ pack.

ONLY 50,000 ABDUCTIONS

Batteries are required. Includes Atlas of Third World

Pat Boone

Fresh from the gene vats to your television screens! Insipid isn't the word – but it's close enough! This one-off singing synthezoid will lull your population into a false sense of complacency. Also eats troublesome small children.

[We regret pupal stage only picture available at present]

ONLY 300,000 ABDUCTIONS
REQUIRES BATTERIES FOR TWO HEARTS.

Artificial Sweetener

Say goodbye sugar and hello Diorybthalmyde-oxidcyclamate Ribothorenenitrate Concentrate! A marvel of technology. Only mildly carcinogenic. Guaranteed only 75ppm urine per serving. Also works as a great rat poison and cleans silverware good as new!

ONLY 150,000 ABDUCTIONS
No batteries required

The Hula Hoop

Is it a Flying Saucer? No, it's a brightly coloured extruded plastic hoop you put around your waist and then gyrate to keep it in place. Why? Who knows? Is it fun? You betcha by golly wow! Wastes hours and hours of time that could otherwise be spent plotting to overthrow the constitutional government of the United States – and will make US companies a large fortune in sales too!

ONLY 200,000 ABDUCTIONS
Does not require batteries

Hydrogen Bomb

Makes the A-Bomb look like a firecracker! Awesome destructive power! Be the first nation on your planet to have one! Taps the same energy as the stars! Devastate cities, continents, etc! Create wastelands! Armageddon has never been so easy! Convenient push-button action!

ONLY 600,000 ABDUCTIONS
Batteries are required
Bomb shown smaller than actual size

Rock 'n' Roll

The very latest in population control – and you've never heard anything like it! A form of music where back-beat meets back-brain. Your rebellious teens will just love this – and it's guaranteed to turn the brightest teenager into a drooling moron! Originally developed by the Syl-Lords of Rigel as a method of rather loud but jolly suicide, Rock 'n' Roll gives the illusion of rebellion, while its invitation to do silly dances and its meaningless lyrics stifle direct political thought and deed! Go on – treat the CIA today!

JUST 500,000 ABDUCTIONS
Does not require batteries

Mulder's video of the alleged Roswell autopsy proved less than convincing. He is adamant that the film is genuine, but I believe that even the briefest perusal of the following stills taken from the film will lead any objective observer to question its authenticity...

Mulder has also forwarded the alleged fragments of the Roswell craft to FBI laboratories for further spectroscopic and metallurgical analysis.

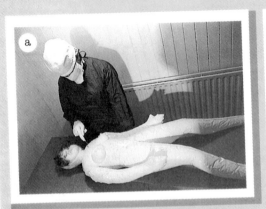

a) THE EBE ALLEGEDLY AWAITING AUTOPSY

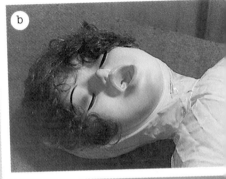

b) CLOSE UP OF EBE CRANIAL REGION

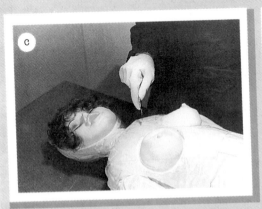

c) ALLEGED GOVERNMENT SCIENTISTS CONDUCT AUTOPSY ON EBE. NOTE 'DEFLATION' EFFECT UPON FIRST SCALPEL INSERTION

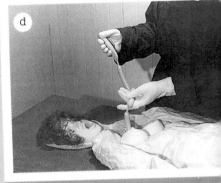

d) ALLEGED ALIEN VISCERA IS REMOVED FROM STOMACH CAVITY. LITTLE RESEMBLANCE TO HUMAN PHYSIOLOGY. EVERY RESEMBLANCE TO PRIME SAUSAGE

To: Dr B Kopitko
From: Agent Mulder

PHOTOGRAPHIC REFERENCE AND SAMPLE SHEET

Please take these four samples h/w for immediate analysis. I
believe they are parts from a flying saucer that crash landed
in the New Mexico desert about fifty years ago.

Look like part of an anti-gravity propulsion system.

Possibly part of the craft's heat shield that became damaged during re-entry

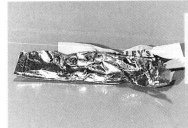

Obviously part of the reactor shielding

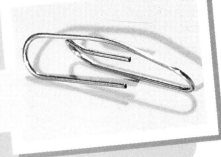

Definitely part of the ionic drive mechanism

WHO KILLED KENNEDY?

X-FILE X-72111

COMPUTER REF: THE MAJIC BULLET

REPORT BY AGENT FOX MULDER

EYES ONLY

It has always been strongly rumoured in UFOlogical circles that President Kennedy was killed because he knew of a secret government conspiracy with EBEs and was about to blow the whistle on it.

I have searched for many years for that tantalising piece of evidence connecting Kennedy to the supposed MJ-12 group, without any success. Meanwhile, my hunt for the elusive assassin (or assassins) continues.

One of my prime suspects over all those years – conveniently left out of the Warren Commission report and Oliver Stone's film – was Frances Gumm, aka 'Judy Garland'. The evidence against her is largely circumstantial, but compelling, and I have started a flow chart to keep track of my investigations... [see right]

I was also convinced that the FBI had also played some role in the President's murder. I checked our employee files for that period. Every single agent had a perfect alibi for the time of the murder. All except one – Special Agent Elvis Aaron Presley.

For some reason, J. Edgar, in his wisdom, had deputised Presley. Perhaps because Elvis was the last person anyone would suspect of putting the fatal shot into Kennedy's head. Now I had the name of a definite FBI suspect, I could look at the evidence in a fresh light and a chilling picture emerged...

Fact!
Fifteen minutes before the shooting, Lee Bowers, stationed in a railroad control tower behind the grassy knoll, saw a man at the stockade fence curl his lip and go 'Uh-huh'.

Fact!
Jack Ruby once remarked to a business associate, 'Wouldn't it be great if I could book Elvis to play at my Carousel Club?'

Fact!
Warren Reynolds chased the killer of Police Officer J D Tippit along Patton Avenue and although he lost him, confirmed that he had supple hips that swung from side to side.

Fact!
Another witness to the Tippit shooting, Domingo Benavides, claimed that the man he saw running away had 'a good head of thick black hair styled in a quiff'.

JUDY GARLAND – THE KENNEDY ASSASSINATION CONNECTION
by FOX MULDER

Wizard of Oz made 1939 ──────▶ Lee Harvey Oswald born 1939

A suburb 10 miles to North East of Dealey Plaza in Dallas = 'Garland'

Kennedy's car drove up Elm Street ──────▶ 'Nightmare on Elm Street' took place in dreams ──────▶ Judy Garland visited Oz in her dreams

Oswald ──────▶ Oz

Jack Ruby ──────▶ Ruby Slippers

Warren Commission ──────▶ Elvira Gulch (not certain)

JFK was KING of 'Camelot' + Martin Luther KING ──────▶ KING VIDOR directed B/W sequence of Wizard of Oz + Mervyn LeRoy (le Roi – the KING) produced Wizard of Oz

Kennedy's brain was shot out ──────▶ The Scarecrow didn't have a brain

Kennedy = Irish descent ──────▶ Emerald City = Irish imagery

EBEs ──────▶ Munchkins

JG (Jim Garrison) ──────▶ JG (Judy Garland)

CIA (three initials) ──────▶ MGM

Kennedy shot ──────▶ 'Ding-Dong! The witch is dead'

Kennedy was crazy about girls ──────▶
Judy Garland appeared in the 1943 film 'Girl Crazy'

Thousands of people cheered Kennedy's motorcade ──────▶ Judy Garland appeared in 1943 musical 'Thousands Cheer'

Judy Garland – Describing what happened to Kennedy's skull?

Triple Underpass in Dallas ──────▶ Yellow Brick Road

Kennedy shot from Texas School*book* Depository ──────▶ 'The Wizard of Oz' was a *book* (published in 1900)

Compelling – but not watertight.

41

Fact!
Rumour has it that Lee Harvey Oswald received a letter from Elvis asking him to audition for the Jordanaires. The letter – now missing – apparently said 'be on the 6th floor of the Schoolbook Depository at 12.30 on 22nd November' and ends 'PS bring a loaded rifle' . (*Right: Elvis Presley – armed and dangerous*)

Fact!
Clay Shaw was an Elvis Presley fan.

Fact!
Some sequins and a rhinestone were apparently found on the 6th floor of the Schoolbook Depository Building – although they do not appear in any inventory of evidence...

Fact!
'Colonel' Tom Parker was a colonel – in the CIA. Other CIA officers with links to the music business have included The *Captain* and Tenille, *Lieutenant* Pigeon, *Captain* Beefheart and *Colonel* Abrahams (LaToya Jackson, although she wears an Admiral's cap, is not understood to have any CIA connections).

Fact!
Presley was drafted into the US Army in 1958 where he learned shooting skills.

Fact!
A man bearing a very close resemblance to Carl Perkins served in the New Orleans Civil Air Patrol alongside Oswald.

Fact!
ELVIS A. PRESLEY is an anagram of SLAYE EVIL PRES (I think Elvis spelled 'slay' with 'e' on the end, which is the olde English preferred spelling).

Fact!
The 'Umbrella Man' in the Zapruder film can be seen wearing blue suede shoes.

Fact!
If you take letters from the following song titles:
'Teddy Bear', 'King Creole', 'Return to Sender', 'Wooden Heart', 'Jailhouse Rock', 'Devil in Disguise' and 'All Shook Up' you can make the phrase:
"I WILL SHOOT KENNEDY IN THE HEAD. CIA GUN PLOT IN DALLAS. DIE JK."
(I admit there are a load of letters left over, but they don't count)

But even if Elvis had been the gunman, he couldn't have acted alone. I ran a computer check on every single one of his known connections. Fifteen hours later, an interesting name cropped up in his fan club membership list, someone who was known to be present on that fateful day – the First Lady, Jackie Kennedy.

Could she have fired the fatal headshot? She was close enough and she did try to flee the scene of the crime over the trunk of the car immediately after the shooting. The president's blood was found on her clothing. Furthermore she had a strong motive. JFK was openly unfaithful to her, as recently released government documents clearly show...

FBI WIRETAP XFS855899
RESIDENCE OF MISS MARILYN MONROE, ACTRESS, LOS ANGELES, CA
5 August 1962. 21.05 Pacific Standard Time.

PRESIDENT KENNEDY: Uh...Hello...Marilyn

MARILYN MONROE: Hi honey. Or should I say Mr President?

PRESIDENT KENNEDY: Is my brother there?

MARILYN MONROE: What's the matter? I'm not good enough for you since you became President, huh? Whatever...I'll put him on.

ROBERT KENNEDY: Jack?

PRESIDENT KENNEDY: Bobby, don't say anything. Marilyn Monroe isn't her real name

ROBERT KENNEDY: I know that, Jack. She's Norma Jean Baker.

PRESIDENT KENNEDY: Brace yourself, Bobby. Marilyn Monroe is actually ██████████████████. Hello? Bobby? Are you still there?

ROBERT KENNEDY: What?

PRESIDENT KENNEDY: She's ████████████ The German ████████████ ████████████ and ████████████.

ROBERT KENNEDY: That's incredible. No Jack, you gotta be wrong about this.

PRESIDENT KENNEDY: On our mother's life, Bobby. Cross my heart and hope to die.

ROBERT KENNEDY: Oh my God! I just ████████████ her.

PRESIDENT KENNEDY: You think that's bad. Last week she ████████ my ████ ████████████████████████ with ████████ and then ████████████████████ Hershey bar.

ROBERT KENNEDY: To think I let her ████████████████████ and even gave her ████████████████ And all the time she was really ████████, leader of the ████████████ party.

PRESIDENT KENNEDY: I bet you didn't ████████████████ ████████████████████ using only ████████.

ROBERT KENNEDY: Jack, we're doing it at the moment. We're doing it as we speak...

PRESIDENT KENNEDY: Pretend you don't know.

ROBERT KENNEDY: That's rather hard, unlike ████████████████! Who else knows? How did you find out?

PRESIDENT KENNEDY: Those ████████████████ at ████████ told me. ████████████████████. We're ████████████, Bobby! When the American people find out that we've both ████████████ Adolf ████████, we're finished!

ROBERT KENNEDY: Don't worry, Jack. Leave it to me...

Every week, we routinely hack into Mulder's X-File on the Kennedy assassination to make sure he hasn't discovered anything remotely like the truth.

He still hasn't. However, his inclusion of the infamous taped Monroe conversations had coincidentally brought him closer to the truth than he had realised...

5 AUGUST 1962

TRANSCRIPT OF MEETING

PRESENT: MEMBERS OF MJ 12
         PRESIDENT JOHN F KENNEDY
         EBE REPRESENTATIVE

1. President Kennedy continued to express his extreme discomfort at the MJ-12 agreement permitting the use of American citizens for alien biological experiments.

"EBEs will abduct Americans over my dead body" Kennedy tells Nixon

2. In a gesture of appeasement, the EBE representative offered him advanced yo-yo technology

3. President Kennedy used the F word and re-emphasised that he was neither Truman nor Eisenhower.

4. Dr Detlev Bronk reminded the President that, since the MJ-12 agreement had been made, America had enjoyed a period of unparalleled wealth and technological advancement.

5. President Kennedy used fourteen different expletives in reply to Dr Bronk's assertion. He said that the American people should be allowed to decide whether or not they wanted to be abducted and used as unwitting hosts for alien foetuses. He officially announced that he will go before the nation soon and the EBEs will have to put their case before the entire American public if they want to continue...

6. There was a long and awkward silence, before Dr Bronk stood and addressed the President as 'you liberal commie pinko faggot'.

7. The President's masculinity was challenged and the entire room fell silent.

8. The President then forced a show of hands to see who around the table from MJ-12 had slept with Marilyn Monroe, Hollywood's greatest sex symbol. Only his hand was raised.

9. A mild level of muffled laughter was perceived in the room, which the President took as doubt of his claim.

10. The President got out personal intimate pictures to prove that he was, indeed, enjoying a full and varied sex life with Miss Monroe.

11. The general level of sniggering increased.

12. General Twining produced hot coffee from both nostrils.

13. The President took this to be further cynicism directed towards his claims and proceeded to describe, in excruciating detail, every single carnal act he and the aforementioned Miss Monroe had ever engaged in.

14. The meeting rapidly disintegrated into uproar. Dr Jerome Hunsaker collapsed and had to be revived with portable oxygen, while General Twining repeatedly banged his head on the desk.

15. Mr William Mulder, egged on by Dr Donald Menzel, then informed the President that Miss Monroe was in fact former Nazi tyrant Adolf Hitler after a complex sex change operation utilising Third Reich and alien genetic engineering procedures.

16. President Kennedy said that he needed to make an urgent phone call and left the meeting.

17. Copies of the agenda were screwed up and thrown at the door after he left. General misbehaviour and merriment ensued.

18. Dr Bronk suggested that MJ-12 employ a top Madison Avenue ad agency to prepare proposals for winning over the American public to the idea of EBEs on earth and their abduction activities.

19. Mr Allen Dulles put the alternative proposal that the President should be shot.

20. It was agreed that both proposals should be explored further.

The meeting was adjourned

CAMPAIGN 1:
Based on patriotism and cold-war paranoia

CAMPAIGN 2:
'Hearts and minds' campaign

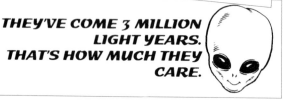

I ♥ BEING ABDUCTED

SAY 'HI' TO YOUR PALS FROM THE SKY

GREYS-THEY'RE CUDDLE-ICIOUS

GRAYS – AS AMERICAN AS APPLE PIE

BALD IS BEAUTIFUL

CAMPAIGN 3:

Target audience: adult males
Objectives: persuade target audience that being abducted makes a man
more successful with women
Media: TV commercial

[A party is in full swing. Jeff is surrounded by beautiful girls and is
holding court. They are laughing and hanging on to his every word.
Two other men, Dave and Steve, are standing outside this group looking on
enviously.]

Dave: Looks like Jeff's the star of the party.

Steve: He always seems to be the centre of attention.

Dave: I just don't know how he does it.

[Jeff leaves the group of girls to get a drink from the bar. On the way back,
Dave stops him.]

Dave: Jeff, how come you get all the prettiest girls?

Jeff: That's easy. Abduction.

Steve: Abduction?

Dave: Like when those aliens take you on board their spacecraft and examine
         you?

Jeff: Sure.

Steve: But doesn't that hurt?

Jeff: Not at all. One minute you're fast asleep, next thing you know you're
         in their spaceship. It couldn't be simpler.

Dave: Sounds like a good idea.

Jeff: It is. Not only that, but they also gave me a free rectal implant!

Girl: [Shouting out] Jeff! We're waiting!

Jeff: Whoops! I'm being summoned fellas. Better go.

[Jeff rejoins the girls.]

Dave: Well. It looks like abduction's good for seduction.

Steve: I'll drink to that!

[Close up of Jeff: he winks at us.]

CAMPAIGN 4:

Target audience: children
Objective: inform target audience, in elementary terms, what an abduction is and why it's not at all scary
Media: children's primer

See the alien. See his funny face. See his funny eyes. Where's his nose? He doesn't have one. Silly alien.

See the light. It is very bright. Even brighter than the sun. If you go in the light you can float. Right up into the sky. Float. Float. Float.

See the alien's spaceship. It can go very fast. Whooooosssshhhh! It can go higher than the moon. Whooooooooosssshhh! Would you like to go for a ride?

Wow! You're in the spaceship. This alien is a dentist. He wants to check your teeth. What a kind alien. Open wide and say 'Aaahhh'. See. Didn't hurt a bit.

CAMPAIGN 5:

Target audience: teenagers
Objective: persuade target audience that EBEs are a trendy, zany, cookie bunch of great guys
Media: recording artists with own TV show

 THE

LYRICS FOR THEME SONG

Here we come
Flying over the street
We take DNA from
Everyone we meet
Hey Hey we're the Grays
People say we're having a laugh
But we're too busy abducting,
Snatching people in our craft.

We are small and we're friendly
We're gray, bald, zany and free
We only like doing fun things
Like proctology...
(Repeat chorus)

POSSIBLE RECORD TITLES
'Last Craft to Saturn'   'Pleasant Implant Sunday'
'A Little Bit Me A Little Bit You'   'I'm a Believer'

:·:·:·:·:·:·:·:
· TOP SECRET ·
:·:·:·:·:·:·:·:

EYES ONLY

CENTRAL INTELLIGENCE AGENCY
Washington 25 DC

From the desk of Allen Dulles

The proposed ad campaign stinks. Go to Plan B. Tell Mia Farrow she's got the green light to go in Dallas.

THE CIA AND THE SUMMER OF LOVE

X-FILE X-71234

COMPUTER REF: YOU SAY YOU WANT A
REVOLUTION

REPORT BY AGENT FOX MULDER

EYES ONLY

On April 21st, purely by chance, I had just left a unisex wig shop when a siege began in the building. Shots were fired. The perpetrator, a Vietnam vet named Gus Banacek, was holding three people hostage and shouting abuse, apparently under the illusion that he was back in Vietnam. He was yelling 'The little men ain't gonna get me again!' and 'all bald wrinkly bastards must die!'

After negotiations failed, a SWAT team rushed him and freed his hostages. Banacek himself sustained minor injuries during the arrest and is now under guard at Mercy County Hospital.

However something he said has set me to thinking...I may be on to something.

The only known picture of Gus Banacek

AGENT SCULLY: What's that you're reading Mulder?

AGENT MULDER: Take a look...

AGENT SCULLY: *Marching Songs of the United States Marine Corps*? Unusual reading, even for you, Mulder. Thinking of joining up?

AGENT MULDER: Listen to this one, Scully.

AGENT SCULLY: This isn't one of those songs that's all about women's private parts, is it Mulder?

AGENT MULDER: Would I? Listen...This is what they were singing out in Vietnam...

Don't send me out on night patrol.
I wanna stay here in my hole.
If I go out in the long tall grass
The little gray men will have my ass.

Sound off!
One, two
Sound off!
Three, four.
One, Two, Three Four, United States Marine
Corps!

I ain't scared of no VC.
It's them that puts the shits up me.
I may have stripes, I may have bars
But they're ugly muthas from the stars.

(Chorus)

They got big black eyes, they got no hair
They fix you with their beady stare.
They pin you down with mind control
And shove a probe right up your hole.

(Chorus)

They got no ears, they got no nose
Their heads are round, they wear no clothes
God's honest truth, I ain't no fool
They strap something on to your tool

(Chorus)

They need you 'cause they cannot mate.
They want your help to procreate.
They fill your head with dirty dreams
'Bout Diana Ross and The Supremes

(Chorus)
They show us scenes of things to come
And treat us like we're awful dumb.

Then they throw us out into the night
Dazed, confused and sick with fright.

(Chorus)

We come back six hours late
And we're still in an awful state.
But when we go to our CO
He says he doesn't want to know.

Sound off!
One, two
Sound off!
Three, four.
One, Two, Three Four, United States Marine
Corps!

AGENT MULDER: What do you think of that Scully?

AGENT SCULLY: It doesn't scan properly.

AGENT MULDER: That's not the point. The point is...

AGENT SCULLY: A lot of experimental toxins were used in Vietnam, Mulder, you know that. It was virtually a testing ground for the CIA. Then you've got herbicides like Agent Orange and Lord only knows what else. The level of serious drug abuse among enlisted men, particularly post 1969, was...

AGENT MULDER: Little men, Scully...

AGENT SCULLY: Remember the 'Sleepless' X-file? Augustus Cole? Remember what you told me they did to him in Vietnam?

AGENT MULDER: Banacek wasn't scared of Charlie. He was scared of being abducted again. Like Duane Barry.

AGENT SCULLY: Duane Barry...

AGENT MULDER: I think we should go and talk to Banacek.

AGENT SCULLY: Duane Barry....

AGENT MULDER: Earth to Scully, Earth to Scully...

AGENT SCULLY: Duane Barry...

AGENT MULDER: I promise I won't let you get kidnapped, abducted by aliens, subjected to alien DNA and left at death's door like last time.

AGENT SCULLY: Duane Barry...

AGENT MULDER: I'll go see him myself. You stay here and...sort out that drooling, OK?

By the time I got to Mercy Hospital, Banacek was dead.

He had died in a mysterious incident involving an elevator shaft, four ginsu knives, one hundred and four .32 calibre bullets, a garotte, enough strychnine to kill a bull elephant, a bull elephant, a speeding dumper truck, twenty-two pounds of gelignite and a vat of industrial acid.

'It was suicide - no doubt about it,' the local police chief told me. 'That man wanted to die - and he wanted to die *real* bad.'

I had the body surrendered into FBI jurisdiction and brought it back for Scully to perform an autopsy...

TRANSCRIPT FROM NSA AUDIO SURVEILLANCE OPERATION:
LOCATION: PATHOLOGY LABORATORIES, FBI BUILDING

AGENT MULDER: Scully, I want you to take a look at these remains.

AGENT SCULLY: Where?

AGENT MULDER: There...

AGENT SCULLY: All I can see is a sort of smudge.

AGENT MULDER: Ten out of ten, Scully. That's all that remains of our Vietnam vet Gus Banacek... Are you feeling OK now? I'm sorry I mentioned Duane Barry.

AGENT SCULLY: Duane Barry...

AGENT MULDER: What are they hiding, Scully? What went on in Vietnam that Banacek remembered and had to be killed for?

AGENT SCULLY: Duane Barry...

AGENT MULDER: Careful, you're drooling on the evidence. Banacek was abducted. Maybe many Vietnam vets were, while they were in country...Why? Scully, why?

AGENT SCULLY: Duane Barry...

In one of his all-too-frequent intuitive leaps, Agent Mulder had uncovered one of our major joint operations with the American humans - the Vietnam War. He had to be put off the scent - before he found out the truth of what had really happened...

PRESIDENTIAL BRIEFING

JULY 7 1964

TOP SECRET / MAJIC
EYES ONLY

TOP SECRET

PRESIDENT L B JOHNSON: They don't want to ride on the backs of buses no more. What are we going to do with the backs of buses in future? Buses'll be 50% empty if negroes won't ride the back.

ASSISTANT DALY: Maybe we can build banana shaped buses, so there's no back?

PRESIDENT L B JOHNSON: Shut up Bill. You may be an ideas man - but your ideas stink.

ASSISTANT DALY: Yes, Mr President. Maybe...we could call the back the front. Or put the driver and the engine at the back, facing backwards and then he could drive backwards and everyone would think the back was the front...

PRESIDENT L B JOHNSON: But then, wouldn't the front be the back?

ASSISTANT DALY: The plan needs developing, OK... It's not perfect. Maybe we could have all-negro buses and all-white buses...

PRESIDENT L B JOHNSON: But then, wouldn't the negroes refuse to ride in the back of the negro buses and the whites refuse to ride in the backs of their buses?

ASSISTANT DALY: What if we made the white and the negro passengers all ride the front of the bus, sitting on each other's laps. The buses would still carry the same amount of people...

PRESIDENT L B JOHNSON: You're fired.

ASSISTANT DALY: Maybe if we gave the negroes bicycles...

PRESIDENT L B JOHNSON: Out, out, out...

ASSISTANT DALY: Yes, Mr President.

PRESIDENT L B JOHNSON: [ON TELEPHONE] Get me MJ-12. I want a meeting out in Dreamland - tomorrow...and I want those tricky little bastards there too...

TOP SECRET EYES ONLY
MJ 12 OPERATION

JULY 8 1964

TRANSCRIPT OF MEETING

PRESIDENT L B JOHNSON: Gentlemen, the country is falling apart. I've got civil rights demonstrations, I got the Black Moslem Movement. I got race riots. I got poverty. I got the Cubans. I got protest singers. I got Beatlemania, for Chrissakes. Everyone knows we did Kennedy...You little gray bastards promised us that, if we got rock 'n' roll going, everyone in this country would be an uncomplaining idiot by 1962!

PRIME GRAY: We have another weapon in our arsenal – bubblegum music. Only 75,000 abduct...

PRESIDENT L B JOHNSON: I don't want to hear it!

PRIME GRAY: You surely don't, Mr President. It sounds awful. The Peach-Men of Deneb...

PRESIDENT L B JOHNSON: Stow it! The CIA says you make half of this shit up anyway! I want a foolproof scheme for getting this country back on its feet – no deals, no payment.

PRIME GRAY: When was your country at its most stable?

PRESIDENT L B JOHNSON: During the last war, I guess...

PRIME GRAY: Then why not have another one...

GENERAL WESTMORELAND: Wahoo! Yes! Yes! Yes! Put it there, gray buddy!

PRESIDENT L B JOHNSON: We could always escalate events in Vietnam.

GENERAL WESTMORELAND: Yeah, get a draft going, get those no good commie-loving punks and uppity negroes shipped out of the country. Do a Field Marshall Haig number on them. Missing generation. Corner of a paddy field that is forever America...sounds appealing, Mr President.

PRIME GRAY: It would suit all our purposes, gentlemen. Your troublesome youth go overseas to die. We can abduct them with far greater ease in the remote terrain (plus being small and smooth-headed, we can disguise ourselves perfectly as Buddhist monks), your industries will benefit from being on a wartime footing and your CIA can experiment with new projects to their heart's content...

GENERAL WESTMORELAND: Please, Mr President. Please please please.

PRESIDENT L B JOHNSON: Get up Willy, it's undignified...OK, we give it a shot. Whoa! Don't kiss me. I don't like being kissed. I just...don't, all right?

Two years later...

TOP SECRET
MJ 12 OPERATION
EYES ONLY

JULY 10 1966

TRANSCRIPT OF MEETING

PRESIDENT L B JOHNSON: War? War? I'll give you war, you stupid gray asshole! You know what they're singing out there? *Hey, hey LBJ, How many kids did you kill today?*

GENERAL WESTMORELAND: In the region of 170, Lyn...

PRESIDENT L B JOHNSON: Shut up, Willy! And don't call me Lyn. Only my wife calls me Lyn. We didn't draft the smart ones. Now they're in college, all reading Chairman Mao and screaming about revolution.

CIA DIRECTOR RICHARD HELMS: I may have just what you're looking for, Mr President. Tell me, have you ever heard of...lysergic acid diethylamide?

Thirty years later, this proved to be rather fortunate for us...

TRANSCRIPT FROM NSA AUDIO SURVEILLANCE OPERATION:
LOCATION: BASEMENT, FBI BUILDING

AGENT MULDER: Cluck-cluck-cluck!

AGENT SCULLY: Take it easy, Mulder!

AGENT MULDER: Cluck! Squawk! Peck-peck-peck...

AGENT SCULLY: Hang on, Mulder!

AGENT MULDER: Scully...Cluck?

AGENT SCULLY: OK, take it easy, Mulder. You're coming out of it now...

AGENT MULDER: So I'm not really a chicken?

AGENT SCULLY: No.

AGENT MULDER: Pity. Right now, I'd kill for an omelette...

AGENT SCULLY: Welcome back, Mulder...

AGENT MULDER: Gee, I think someone must have slipped me something. Did I...did I do anything embarrassing?

AGENT SCULLY: Where do you think your pants are, Mulder?

AGENT MULDER: What did I do?

AGENT SCULLY: You mean, you don't remember perching on Skinner's desk and trying to lay an egg in his drawer?

AGENT MULDER: I didn't, did I?

AGENT SCULLY: Yup. But...it wasn't an egg, Mulder.

AGENT MULDER: Someone slipped me Acid, Scully. Maybe it's a warning...or maybe someone's trying to tell me something.

AGENT SCULLY: So, what's it like being a chicken?

AGENT MULDER: The feathers kinda tickle...

AGENT SCULLY: Try to get some rest, Mulder - and then go and apologise to Skinner. I'm going to look into this...

TRANSCRIPT FROM NSA AUDIO SURVEILLANCE OPERATION:
LOCATION: BASEMENT, FBI BUILDING

AGENT SCULLY: I've cracked it, Mulder!

AGENT MULDER: Oh no, my egg! My precious, beautiful egg. Er...sorry, Scully. Flashback...

AGENT SCULLY: There were no aliens in Vietnam to abduct Gus Banacek or anyone else. It was the CIA. In late 1966, their MK-ULTRA program had decided to use lysergic acid diethylamide on American kids.

AGENT MULDER: LSD, huh. What was that? Oh no! It's Colonel Sanders! Ahhh! God, I'm sorry, Scully Another flashback...

AGENT SCULLY: The Government of the time were concerned about youth rebellion. It looked like there was going to be a revolution, so the CIA took to the streets, made cheap LSD the drug of choice and fried everyone's brains. While you're tripping, you're not rebelling, right?

AGENT MULDER: Where's the evidence for this Scully? Where'd you get this?

AGENT SCULLY: From your friend Frohike. I think he likes me...

AGENT MULDER: Want me to fix you up on a date, Scully?

AGENT SCULLY: He gave me this. Do you know who these men are?

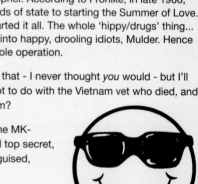

AGENT MULDER: One half of Country Joe and the Fish?

AGENT SCULLY: The one on the left is CIA operative Richard Stark. On the right is CIA man James Earl Christopher. According to Frohike, in late 1966, early 1967 these two went from assassinating foreign heads of state to starting the Summer of Love. Just look at the CIA materials of the time Mulder. They started it all. The whole 'hippy/drugs' thing... They were turning the finest young minds of a generation into happy, drooling idiots, Mulder. Hence the sick symbol – the smiley – they concocted for the whole operation.

AGENT MULDER: OK, I'll buy that - I never thought *you* would - but I'll buy that. But what's that got to do with the Vietnam vet who died, and reports of aliens in Vietnam?

AGENT SCULLY: While the MK-ULTRA operation was still top secret, they kept the 'Smiley' disguised, Mulder. Look at this...

AGENT SCULLY: This is what those soldiers were seeing, Mulder. Look, the dark big eyes, the bald head. No ears, no nose. They were kidnapped by the CIA, Mulder. They were perfecting LSD use on soldiers before they released it on the streets of America.

AGENT MULDER: So, no aliens. That's an ingenious theory, Scully. But where's the proof?

AGENT SCULLY: There isn't any, Mulder. As usual. Only *he* knows the real truth - and he's not telling...

CIA NEWS LETTER

SUMMER OF 1967

TURN ON, TUNE IN AND SHOOT SOMEONE!

FEED YOUR HEAD (OF SECTION)

YOUR ART AND POETRY – INSIDE!

ALL YOU NEED IS LOVE (AND A MAUSER WITH A SILENCER!)

HIPPY CHICK OF THE WEEK! YOW!

We love you yeah yeah yeah, Senior Field Director (Central America) Sally Lipschwitz. Shake that love thing!

A POEM

I was a wardrobe
Or maybe I wasn't.
I might have been something else.
Or maybe not.

— Richard Helms, Director,
Central Intelligence Agency

Wow! Groooooovy new staff cars are killer!

KEEP ON ASSASSINATIN'

LOVE IN

Room 401, Langley HQ. 4.30 Friday after target practice. Be there or be square.

NIXON AND THE NEW WORLD ORDER

Surprising as it may seem, Agent Mulder's responsibility wasn't solely to investigate X-Files. He was trained to help capture serial killers by 'profiling' them, and had written a paper on 'Serial Killers and the Occult'.

Given the situation in modern day America, tracking down mass murderers also took up much of his time...

OPERATION MAJESTIC 12

**TOP SECRET
MJ 12 OPERATION** EYES ONLY

FEBRUARY 10TH 1973

TRANSCRIPT OF MEETING

RICHARD HELMS: As the head of the CIA and your most trusted adviser...

PRESIDENT RICHARD NIXON: I've never seen you before in my life, buster!

RICHARD HELMS: Of course not, Mr President.

PRESIDENT RICHARD NIXON: And I'm not the President. I'm Marie Osmond.

RICHARD HELMS: Of course, Mr President. Now as I was saying, MK-ULTRA has allowed us to create many ruthless assassins...

PRIME GRAY: Mr President, you are not wise to follow this course...

RICHARD HELMS: Shut it, shorty. There's a dissection table with your name on it at Wright-Patterson.

PRIME GRAY: Ulp...

WILLIAM MULDER: This is an abomination! I've gone along with a lot, closed my eyes to so much over the years, because I thought it was in the best interests of the country... But I won't be a party to this! I quit – and if you go ahead with this, I swear I'll expose you.

MR MULDER LEAVES THE ROOM

RICHARD HELMS: He has two children sir. Fox and Samantha.

PRESIDENT RICHARD NIXON: Well, I don't think we should get our Gray friends here to kidnap either of them to ensure Mr Mulder's silence...

RICHARD HELMS: We'll get on to it right away sir – won't we, Shorty?

REFRESHMENT TROLLEY ENTERS

John Wayne Gacy on his graduation day. Congratulated by First Lady Rosalyn Carter.

Cont.

Cont.

PRESIDENT RICHARD NIXON: Ah, the refreshments have not arrived!

SECRETARY: Would you like some coffee, Mr President?

PRESIDENT RICHARD NIXON: No.

SECRETARY: How many sugars?

PRESIDENT RICHARD NIXON: Four million.

SECRETARY: Cream?

PRESIDENT RICHARD NIXON: No, it's not. It's a car. And I'm not the president. I'm Jon Voight.

SECRETARY: Very good, Mr President.

RICHARD HELMS: We can do so much more with this. Create murderers, violent criminals. Scare the American people so badly that they'll beg us to suspend the constitution and get down and lick our jackboots when we do so...

PRESIDENT RICHARD NIXON: I absolutely forbid you to do this!

RICHARD HELMS: I'll get right on to it, sir.

PRESIDENT RICHARD NIXON: God, I love this country!

X-FILE: X-78598
COMPUTER REF: MILLENNIAL RIGHTS
REPORT BY AGENT FOX MULDER
EYES ONLY

My days at college in Oxford were some of the happiest of my life.

I had my studies, I had sports and I had Phoebe (until she caught me in her New Romantic pirate boots, white leggings and cerise bra top - damn that alien transvestite ray which has plagued my life for so very long...)

After I left, I never dreamed I would ever find myself back in school again...

This morning, I found two newspaper cuttings have been passed under my door. One was about serial killer Jeffrey Dahmer, the other Ted Bundy. Someone was trying to tell me something. Why they have to be so cryptic I don't know. It pisses me off.

On a hunch, I laboured all morning on the computer, looking for possible connections between the two. I eventually found an interesting correlation - both had attended a college called 'The Richard Nixon Academy' in Salem, Massachusetts. On a hunch, I checked out the records of several other convicted serial killers. 'The Richard Nixon Academy' turned up on every single one...

I was on to something. I went straight down to the library and filled in an application form for the academy...

COLLEGE APPLICATION FORM

NAME: Fox 'The Cannibal' Mulder

AGE: 35

ADDRESS: Apartment 42, 3412 West St, Alexandria, VA

QUALIFICATIONS:

Ownership of a bandsaw and axe. Extensive severed head collection.

PERSONAL INTERESTS AND HOBBIES:

Self-mutilation. Necrophagia, playing basketball with severed heads, taunting the police in sixteen states, making severed toe vol-au-vents (samples available on request). Drooling while staring off into space.

COURSE APPLIED FOR: PhD Serial Killing

FRAT/SORORITY SOUGHT: Phi Alpha Bloodbath

REASONS WHY YOUR APPLICATION SHOULD BE CONSIDERED:

I am diagnosed as paranoid schizophrenic and I like to cook and eat nuns. I threw my parents off a cliff and I want to sleep with Roseanne Barr.

PROPOSED METHOD OF FINANCE:
Marrying and then butchering aged heiresses.

OTHER COLLEGES APPLIED FOR:

1. The Calvin Coolidge School of Advanced Spree Killing
2. Woodrow Wilson College (Faculty of Mass Murder)
3. The McKinley School for the Advancement of Random Slayings
4. The Gerald Ford Foundation (Faculty of Shooting All Your Workmates)
5. Harvard Business School (Department of Advanced Management Studies - And a Bit of Killing)

PLEASE PROVIDE TWO REFERENCES

Dana 'The Biter' Scully
3170 W. 53 Rd. #35
Annapolis, MD

Walter 'Skinner' Skinner
1514 Elm Street
Chevy Chase, MD

At three o'clock the next morning, I was dragged out of bed by an armed SWAT team...

I had accidentally filled in the Yale College entrance form by mistake.

Skinner vouched for me and I was eventually released. They tell me I might also get my videos back if they're not destroyed.

Undeterred, I decided to visit the 'Richard Nixon Academy' undercover. The moment I arrived at the college, I could smell the evil. It was a strange, twisted place. The students were dull-eyed, restless, shambling mockeries of men and women, constantly drinking, doing drugs, screaming at all hours of the night. I saw every form of sexual act imaginable performed in plain sight. I felt the hatred, the madness and the depravity like a physical blow.

It was three days before I realised I'd joined the University of Massachusetts by mistake, and that the Richard Nixon Academy was ten miles further down the road, behind some trees.

I went down there the very next day and applied for the student body. (The student body, as it turned out, was a 59-year-old shoe salesman from Kentucky unlucky enough to have given someone a ride while crossing Iowa... Apparently another student was using it, but it was due back Friday.)

I decided not to join a Fraternity, as the 'hazing' initiation ritual involved being killed and having your bowels buried in six non-adjoining states of the Union.

Instead I settled in, watching, taking notes, attending classes on how to bite off ears, how not to bathe for months at a time and how to compose rambling, badly spelled notes to the police. I took photographs, tried out for the Head hockey team and won the spelling bee with the correct spelling of *Viscera*. I went through college files and found the school was affiliated with other 'crime academies' throughout the country. What's more, they were all funded by central government. Every single one of them. Then, I got a note from X under my dorm room door, telling me to meet him in the car park of the Watergate Hotel...

ALUMNI
ACADEMY HALL OF FAME

JEFFREY DAHMER - 'The Quiet One'

Axe Club. Gay Club:

VOTED: 'STUDENT MOST LIKELY TO HAVE COLD CUTS IN THE ICE BOX IF YOU DROP OVER UNEXPECTEDLY'

'MAD MITCH' MINGUS

Impaling Club: Garotte semi-finalist.

VOTED: 'STUDENT MOST LIKELY TO DIE IN A HAIL OF POLICE BULLETS'

CHARLES MANSON - 'Shorty'

Music Club.

VOTED: 'STUDENT MOST LIKELY TO COP AN INSANITY PLEA'

LUCY BATES - 'Juicy Lucy'

Gun club: Cookery: Larceny Ed.

VOTED: 'PERSON MOST LIKELY TO GET THEIR OWN TV MINI SERIES'

TED BUNDY - 'Smiley'

First Aid Society.

VOTED: 'STUDENT MOST LIKELY TO FOOL THE COPS'

SHAUN O'GRADY - 'Monster'

Biting club: Dismemberment Ed.

VOTED 'STUDENT MOST LIKELY TO INSPIRE THE RETURN OF THE DEATH PENALTY IN ALL 52 STATES'

JOHN WAYNE GACY - 'Class Clown'

Art Class: Film Club: Inter-Sodomy Football Team (Wide Receiver).

VOTED: 'BIGGEST SLOB IN SCHOOL'

DAVID BERKOWITZ - 'Fatty'

VOTED: 'STUDENT MOST LIKELY TO HEAR VOICES AND DO SOMETHING UTTERLY DERANGED'

CHARLES STOTT - 'Crazy Charlie'

Biting Club: Club Club

VOTED: 'STUDENT I'D LEAST TRUST WITH AN ICE PICK'

X-FILE: X-78598

COMPUTER REF: MILLENNIAL RIGHTS

REPORT BY AGENT FOX MULDER

EYES ONLY

'X' met me in the deserted underground car park. One moment I was alone, the next minute he had stepped out of the darkness and was beside me.

'Drop it, Mulder,' he barked. 'School's out!'

'Gee, I nearly made the team,' I replied, determined not to be intimidated.

'You're not hearing me, Agent Mulder,' X said, pushing me back against the car.

'I want to know why the government is sponsoring a school for serial murderers!' I shouted, pushing him back. 'I want to know why they've got affiliate schools for robbers, muggers, rapists, gangbangers, vandals, carjackers, car thieves...'

'Forget it, Mulder. Drop out. Go home! That's an order! The college is closed now. Gone. If you tell anyone, it won't be there. It's all taken care of. Now relax! Unwind...Go take in a show...'

He handed me a theatrical handbill, then faded back into the darkness. I heard his footsteps fading away, then a muffled thud and a cry of pain. Then a few more footsteps, then the sound of someone falling heavily, followed quickly by furious swearing.

Working in the shadows obviously has its disadvantages...

THE BILL CLINTON DANCERS!
APPEARING ALL OVER AMERICA FROM THE YEAR 2000!

You know you want them...

EXCLUSIVE PREVIEWS BY INVITATION ONLY!

A New World Order Production.
Stomp! receives generous financial assistance from the Federal Government.

AGENT MULDER

As soon as we realised the potential threat Agent Mulder posed to us, we initiated an intensive campaign of harassment and disinformation directed at him.

Sometimes our intention was to actually drive him mad. Sometimes we attempted to make him appear mad to his colleagues (not the hardest of tasks).

However, simply wasting Mulder's time, and filling his life with petty distractions and annoyances also proved effective and, strangely, quite satisfying...

SPECIAL OPERATIONS
METHOD 1: RING MULDER'S DOORBELL AND RUN AWAY

Despite giving this seemingly simple task to our own elite Special Operations Experts, they experienced nothing but problems in carrying it out...

REPORT TO PRIME GRAY FROM SPECIAL OPERATIONS

MISSION A

Attempt 1 - Went up to Mulder's door and waited there, having forgotten what to do next. Went back to spacecraft.

Attempt 2 - Went back to Mulder's door and then realised that I couldn't reach the bell. Went back to spacecraft to get a chair.

Attempt 3 - Went back to the door but then realised that I'd left the chair in the spacecraft. Back to spacecraft.

Attempt 4 - Went back to the door and ran away, having forgotten to ring the bell. Went back to find that chair had been stolen. Back to spacecraft to get a replacement.

Attempt 5 - Went back to the door with replacement chair, was about to ring bell when a neighbour came out of her apartment and I had to run away.

Attempt 6 - Went back to the door, only to find that the second chair had been stolen. Back to spacecraft to get another one. (By now two of the crew are standing and complaining of aching feet.)

Attempt 7 - Went back to door but fell off chair during attempt to ring the bell and hurt my arm. Went back to spacecraft (remembered to take chair back with me this time).

Attempt 8 - Went back to door. Stood on chair. Because it was one of our

chairs, it still wasn't high enough for me to reach the bell. Stood on tip toes.
Fell over. Went back to spacecraft.

Attempt 9 - Got back to Mulder's with new chair. Relieved to find first one still
there. Put new chair on top of first chair and climbed up to ring bell. Nothing
happened. Rang again but nothing happened. Slipped note through Mulder's
door saying that his bell needed new batteries, hoping he acts on this advice.

Attempt 10 - Following day, went up to door with both chairs. Succeeded in
ringing bell at first attempt but forgot to run away. Mulder opened door right
in my face, knocking me to the ground. Managed to limp back to spacecraft
without being seen.

Attempt 11 - Flushed with near success I repeated exercise, determined to
remember to run away this time. Rang bell. Mulder opened door before I could
climb down from precariously stacked chairs. Sent flying. Managed to limp
back to spacecraft without being seen.

CONCLUSION - Wasted far more of my time than I did of his.

MISSION B (To set alight bag of canine excrement material outside Agent Mulder's
door, thereby inviting him to stamp on it and ruin his shoes).

Attempt 1 - Went up to door (with chairs) put bag on step. Realised I'd forgotten
to fill it with dog dirt. Went back to spacecraft.

Attempt 2 - Went back to door with bag of dog dirt but forgot matches. Went
back to spacecraft.

Attempt 3 - Dropped bag of dog dirt in spacecraft just as I was leaving. Got
shouted at (telepathically).

Attempt 4 - Went back to door with new bag of dog dirt and matches.
Accidentally dropped matches in bag of dog dirt. Did not feel inclined to
retrieve them. Went back to spacecraft.

Attempt 5 - Went back to door with new matches and bag of dog dirt. Put bag on
step. Dog from neighbouring apartment came up and started sniffing the bag,
then chased me.

Attempt 6 - Returned to door with matches and bag of dog dirt. Checked no
dogs were present, put bag on step, set fire to it and ran away. Half-way along
corridor, realised that I had forgotten to ring bell. Ran back and stamped on
bag to put it out. Messed own footwear irreparably.

Attempt 7 - Went back to door with fresh matches, fresh footwear and new bag
of dog dirt. Put bag on step, set fire to it, arranged chairs on top of one
another and climbed up to reach bell. Before I could ring the bell, flames from
the bag set fire to the bottom chair and I had to jump off. Fell on bag which
burst, covering me with dog dirt. Fire set off sprinkler system. Got soaked.
Went back to spacecraft but they wouldn't let me in.

CONCLUSION - Get the CIA to do this kind of job in future.

This proved to be a particularly effective way of wasting Mulder's time. No sooner would he sit down at home to work on a case when his phone would ring. And ring. And ring...

These are the sort of advertisements we found most effective...

UFO ABDUCTIONS!

I want to hear from anyone who's been abducted by aliens, no matter how stupid their story might sound, like even if all the aliens looked like Barney or David Letterman. In fact, the more the bizarre the story the better! Even if you haven't actually been abducted, but dream about it, ring me as well and we can share fantasies (I've got this one about being beamed up to a UFO and having a huge rectal probe slowly inserted then twisted to the sounds of 'Star Spangled Banner'). I'm waiting to hear from you!

Call Fox on (202) 555-9355

Want to fly in a UFO?

I work for the Government investigating UFOs and am able to pull a few strings to get you the flight of your life - on board a genuine UFO! That's right, for only $50 you can have a twenty minute flight to Saturn and back, buzz some F-16s and put the wind up air traffic controllers nationwide.

You'll also be given a guided tour of the craft and have your photo taken with a Gray. This is a serious offer but hurry, places are limited!

Call Fox on (202) 555-9355

Are you a Mole Man?

Did you know that moles aren't pigmentation defects but, in fact, the sign that you've been abducted and there's a small alien implant under your skin. I have a mole on my right cheek and doctors found a miniature tracking device under it! If you have a mole anywhere on your entire body you must contact me immediately!!!

Call Fox on (202) 555-9355

Desperately seeking Samantha

I'm looking for my sister who was abducted by aliens in 1973, aged 9. I don't know what you look like now but if you're reading this please contact me. Father died and there's a $1.5 million inheritance waiting for you.

Call Fox Mulder on (202) 555-9355

This is just a sample of the many thousands of letters Mulder subsequently received...

Dear Agent Mulder,
We are all being poisoned. Butter is the Devil's semenal fluid and when we eat it we go mad and do things like chop up our mothers because she won't stop talking and then hiding her remains in the cellar behind a box of old newspapers, the bitch!

yours,
Paul Felton.

P.s. It also raises your cholesteral levels.

dere agunt muldy
mi wyf is a wich can you shuut her?

Billy-Bob
tornado trayler park
alabamma
I am not crazee

Dear mr Mulder
I think my son is possessed by the demon Pazuzu, like in The Exorcist. He screams and cries and wails and wets himself. Sometimes, he also vomits on me. When he is not doing this he stares into space and talks a weird kind of unearthly gibberish. Why did the Lord allow this to happen to my son? He's only a year old for God's sake?

Dear Agent Mulder.
I think we are descended from the bees.
I just think we are.

Lawrence xxxx

DEAR AGENT MULDER

LAST NIGHT, SPACE ALIENS
KIDNAPPED ME AND REMOVED MY
ARMS AND LEGS, THEN THEY PUT
THEM ON EXACTLY THE SAME WAY
AGAIN, SO NO ONE WOULD BELIEVE ME,
CAN YOU HELP ME?

      YOURS

        RICHARD PARKER

P.S. I KNOW WHO THEIR LEADER
IS, IT IS STEVE GUTTENBERG.

TRANSCRIPT FROM NSA SURVEILLANCE OPERATION:
LOCATION: BASEMENT, FBI BUILDING

AGENT MULDER: Did you place this ad, Scully?

AGENT SCULLY: No.

AGENT MULDER: Strange. Maybe X did it. We're going to investigate every one of these cases, Scully, starting with this one...

Dear Mr Mulder,

Please do not think I am mad but my husband, my relations and my friends are all starting to act very odd indeed. They talk on the phone when they think I'm not there and have secret meetings. When I question my husband, he gets very strange and pretends nothing is going on.

I want the man I married back. Can you help me?

Yours,

E. Kropotkin.

Kropotkin, E.G (Mrs)

X-FILE X77011
COMPUTER REF: SLEEPLESS IN SEATTLE
REPORT BY AGENT FOX MULDER
EYES ONLY

I recognised what was going on immediately I received the letter.

How could I tell Mrs Kropotkin that her husband, her friends and loved ones had all been consumed by the pods while they slept and that vegetable based duplicates were now walking around in their place, scheming their cold floronic schemes?

When I told Scully we had to rush to Seattle to prevent an invasion by extra-terrestrial vegetable entities, she made some unconvincing excuse and left. Not Scully too, please God!

The next week was a nightmare. I barely remember anything that happened, because I dared not sleep at all. All I know is that I am back in my office, with Mrs Kropotkin in protective custody, and I am in trouble with Assistant Director Skinner.

He summoned me to see him the moment I returned. I studied him hard. Had they got him too? My heart leapt when he raised his arm and opened his mouth. For a moment, I thought he was going to make the strange ultra-sonic warning noise 'pod-people' use to identify strangers, but instead he was just speechless with rage and frantically gesturing for me to get out...

Dear Assistant Director Skinner,

I wish to make an official complaint about one of your men, a Special Agent Fox Mulder, badge number JTT047101111.

From the moment he moved into our home, he was rude, aggressive and obnoxious, deliberately trying to goad me and insisting on referring to me as 'Pod-Boy'.

As the week progressed, his behaviour became more and more erratic. He refused to sleep, staying awake by playing loud rock music, watching scary horror films and taking pills. On more than one occasion, I witnessed him slapping my wife repeatedly, ordering her not to fall asleep.

Things finally reached a head last Saturday, when Agent Mulder leapt out of our closet, sprayed me with a cheap herbicide and then took a baseball bat to my prized giant watermelon collection.

To add insult to injury, he then ran screaming through our street covered in watermelon juice, yelling, 'They're here! You're next! They come when you sleep!', jumping on several parked cars and damaging them in the process.

Now he has snatched my wife and won't say where she is. For weeks now, her family and friends and I having been planning a secret grand surprise 50th birthday party for her. Now it's all ruined...

METHOD 3: CONVINCE HIM TO PUT STRANGE ITEMS IN HIS WINDOW

Once we sent him this note, ostensibly from 'X'...

Special Agent Mulder,

I have to ask you to change strategy. For reasons too complicated to go into I want you to cease requesting my presence by taping a large 'X' on your apartment window. Instead, place any of the following there and I will come out of the shadows to respond.

a) A notice that says 'Free drugs here!'

b) A red lamp and a sign that says 'Big Beefy Truckers: $10 for a hand job'

c) A sign that says 'I've killed my male lover and he's under the floorboards'

d) Your face, pressed hard against the glass with your tongue half sticking out

e) Your buttocks, pressed hard against the glass

f) A sign that says 'Are you a vagrant? Free bath, hot soup and a bed for the night. Come in - all welcome (also, de-licing)'

g) A sign that says 'Room to rent. $2 a month all inclusive. Mentally challenged and recently paroled violent offenders welcomed'

h) A Playmate of the month centrefold, with the Reverend Louis Farrakhan's head pasted on to it

From time to time we used to drop sheets like these through Mulder's letterbox, to play on his strongly competitive streak and his love of solving mysteries. By all accounts, he spent days fruitlessly trying to figure out these impossible games.

X-FILES ACTIVITY SHEET

1. Help the EBE find his way back to his UFO

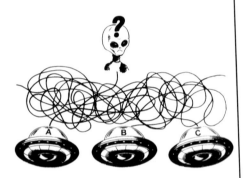

2. Can you get from VAMPIRE to BIGFOOT in seven stages, just by changing one letter at a time?

V   A   M   P   I   R   E
....
....
....
....
....
B   I   G   F   O   O   T

3. If EBE 1 travels from Neptune to the Earth at the speed of light but stops off at Saturn for three days, and EBE 2 travels from Earth to Neptune at two thirds the speed of light but does not stop, how far away from the Earth (to the nearest mile) will they be when they meet?

4. Which two pictures of Saturn are identical?

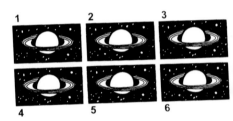

5. EBE 1 mutilates half the number of sheep that EB 2 mutilates, and three times as many cows as EBE mutilates. EBE 2 mutilates half the number of goats that EBE 3 mutilates but only one quarter of the co that EBE 1 mutilates. If EBE 1 mutilates 15 cows a 28 goats and EBE 3 mutilates 18 sheep, how mar cows, goats and sheep has EBE 2 mutilated?

6. How many words of seven letters or more can make from 'OPERATION PAPERCLIP' (no foreign words or proper nouns)

7. John's watch runs twenty minutes fast, Jack's is fifteen minutes slow and Jill's gains a minute ever hour. All three are abducted at midnight but on board the UFO, time for them is slowed to one-fi the normal speed. When they are released John watch says 6.15am.

a) How long were they actually on board the UF
b) What time would be shown on Jack's watch?
c) How long will it take for Jill's watch to show th correct time?

METHOD 5: LEAVE ANONYMOUS NOTES TO PUT HIM OFF THE TRAIL

Pushing a few anonymous notes under Mulder's door quickly drove him to hitherto unreached heights of paranoia...

THE TRUTH IS IN YOUR BREADBOX

We know!

Deny everything (except your chronic body odour problem)

The truth is... Oh dear, my pen's run out

The truth is sfsgzxdkwhy!

The truth is out there (turn left on the corner, then second right, hang a left, continue past the stop sign and carry on until the next junction)

THE TRUTH IS 23

The CIA, Com-12, Aquarius, Masons, P2, Green Dragon Society, the Order of the Golden Dawn, Org, Priory of Sion, Knights Templars, New World Order Trilaterists, Vatican and the Military-Industrial Complex called to reveal the truth - but you were out.

Stop it! You'll go blind!

METHOD 6: LEAVE A CODED MESSAGE FOR HIM IN NAVAJO:

On several occasions, we left a cryptic note in Navajo under Mulder's door. Typically, it said something like...

'el 'aanidgo 'ahoot'e hoa 'ordta 'aosoo aeoo 'aoohot ehaat 'iroode iireoat 'aanigo 'eehsteo eeiori 'aeeidtho auddi'

He always assumed that it was a top secret message about Majestic 12 in Navajo and jumped on a plane to the nearest Navajo reservation to get it translated.

The message was always in Navajo - but never about UFOs. It usually translated to something like:

'I hate you pesky redskinned varmits and General Custer was a great guy. Kiss my palefaced butt, Cochise'

Six times we put him through this ordeal. Six times he completely fell for it. Special Agent Mulder was beaten twice, staked-out on an ant hill three times and tarred and feathered once.

METHOD 7: HUMILIATE HIM IN FRONT OF COLLEAGUES AND SUPERIORS

WHEREVER POSSIBLE

J EDGAR JAMBOREE!
by invitation only

YOU ARE INVITED TO A DAY-LONG CELEBRATION OF THE LIFE AND ACHIEVEMENTS OF A TRUE AMERICAN HERO - J. EDGAR HOOVER, THE GREATEST FBI MAN OF ALL TIME (AND FEARLESS CROSS DRESSER)!

DRESS: Women's Evening Wear mandatory for all male agents
VENUE: Department of Behavioural Psychology
TIME: From 8.30am. Prompt attendance please!

F.B.I.

NOTIFICATION OF COMPULSORY MEDICAL

NAME: SPECIAL AGENT FOX MULDER
BADGE NUMBER: JTT047101111

Please attend for a medical next Monday morning at 8.30 am, stripped to underwear.

VENUE: ASSISTANT DIRECTOR SKINNER'S OFFICE

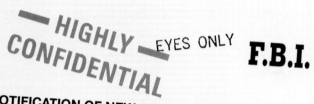

HIGHLY CONFIDENTIAL — EYES ONLY

F.B.I.

NOTIFICATION OF NEW ASSIGNMENT

A number of serious felony assaults have recently been reported at the 'Fairytaleland' Amusement Park. You and Agent Scully are assigned to the case in an undercover capacity.

Please disguise yourself as a suitable fairytale character. You may choose between Little Bo Beep, Humpty Dumpty and Little Red Riding Hood.

Please report to my office for a full briefing first thing Monday in costume.

WwS.

Walter S Skinner
Assistant Director

TRANSCRIPT FROM NSA SURVEILLANCE OPERATION:
LOCATION: BASEMENT, FBI BUILDING

AGENT MULDER: I just don't get it, Scully?

AGENT SCULLY: What Mulder?

AGENT MULDER: How Pamela Anderson can be having Elvis's love child? The very same newspaper said that the the ghost of Elvis had been dictating new songs to a woman in Iowa...

AGENT SCULLY: Are you reading the *National Enquirer* again, Mulder?

AGENT MULDER: This is where I get most of our cases from, Scully. Someone's subscribed on our behalf. I think it's X - tipping us off...

AGENT SCULLY: Mulder, they make it all up in there.

AGENT MULDER: Scepticism is the sign of a closed mind.

AGENT SCULLY: Mulder, you'll believe anything. I bet you still believe in Santa Claus.

AGENT MULDER: He exists, Scully.

AGENT SCULLY: Right.

AGENT MULDER: No, wait, when Samantha and I were little, he came every Christmas morning and left our presents under the tree. We both witnessed it. And how do you explain all the millions of others all around the world who independently report mysterious parcels being left in stockings or under trees?

AGENT SCULLY: Mulder, Santa Claus...how do I tell you this? Santa Claus was your dad.

(SILENCE)

AGENT MULDER: Scully, do you realise what this means?

AGENT SCULLY: You're crazier than I thought?

AGENT MULDER: Agent Krycek killed...Santa Claus. That bastard...

AGENT SCULLY: Mulder, when I said your father...

AGENT MULDER: Now it all makes sense...

AGENT SCULLY: Only to a diseased mind.

AGENT MULDER: No, Scully, listen. We know my father was involved with the EBEs and in handling 'the merchandise'. It's almost the last thing he told me. What if he was referring to...the presents? Legends say that Santa is assisted in his workshop by dwarves - little men, Scully. Why didn't I see this before?

AGENT SCULLY: And how did your father manage to visit all the children of the world in one night, Mulder?

AGENT MULDER: It all makes sense - if he had access to alien technology. Maybe it was a retro engineered saucer from Dreamland, Scully. Maybe he used some kind of 'time dilation effect' like the aliens to stretch Christmas Eve out.

AGENT SCULLY: Mulder, your father was...elderly. How did he squeeze down the chimneys?

AGENT MULDER: My God - he was working with Eugene Tooms.

AGENT SCULLY: Don't be ridiculous.

AGENT MULDER: It's the only explanation, Scully. My father drove the 'sleigh', Tooms came down the chimney.

AGENT SCULLY: If you keep talking like this, I'm going to get my mace spray out. You're starting to scare me, Mulder.

AGENT MULDER: You know, it's always bothered me, *'he knows if you are sleeping, he knows when you're awake'*. Thats how the rhyme went. *'He knows if you've been bad or good.'* Scully, the kids all have implants! That's how he knew!

SPRAYING SOUND

AGENT MULDER: ARRRGHHH!

AGENT SCULLY: It's for your own good, Mulder. Now calm down. Listen to me and repeat. There-is-no-Santa-Claus.

AGENT MULDER: Of course not. Krycek killed him...

SPRAYING SOUND

AGENT MULDER: ARRRGHHH!

ASSISTANT DIRECTOR SKINNER: Agent Scully...what are you doing?

AGENT SCULLY: Macing Mulder, sir.

ASSISTANT DIRECTOR SKINNER: Good work. I'll come back later...

BILL MULDER,
EX-US STATE
DEPARTMENT

LAYOUT OF HIS APARTMENT

(This involved a considerable expenditure of energy to dissolve and reconstruct his entire apartment on a sub-molecular level, but it worked exceptionally well. Numerous visitors to Mulder's apartment said how it never appeared the same twice)

Day 1

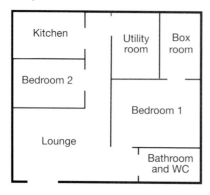

Day 2

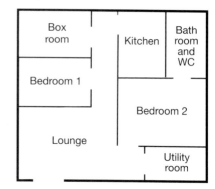

Day 3

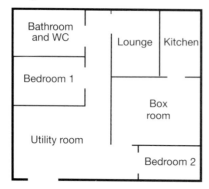

Day 4

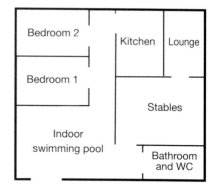

Day 5

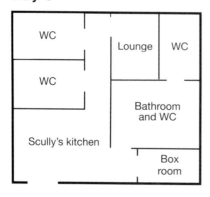

METHOD 10: USE HIS MISSING SISTER TO MANIPULATE HIM

Agent Mulder's true Achilles' heel was his missing sister, Samantha. He would believe absolutely anything about her and go to absolutely any length in his quest to find her...

TRANSCRIPT FROM NSA SURVEILLANCE OPERATION:
LOCATION: BASEMENT, FBI BUILDING:

BANG!

AGENT MULDER: Owww!

BANG!

AGENT MULDER: OWWW!

BANG!

AGENT MULDER: Owww!

AGENT SCULLY: I'm sorry, Mulder, the canteen was all out of diet soda...

BANG!

AGENT MULDER: Owww!

AGENT SCULLY: Mulder, what's wrong? What are you doing?

AGENT MULDER: I'm trying to knock out some of my teeth, Scully.

BANG!

AGENT MULDER: Owww!

AGENT SCULLY: Stop it! Stop it! Why Mulder, why?

AGENT MULDER: I want to do a surveillance operation on the tooth fairy.

BANG!

AGENT MULDER: Owww!

AGENT SCULLY: Wait, whoa, whoa, whoa. Let's talk this over. You're bleeding. It's awful. What gave you this...idea?

AGENT MULDER: I remembered. Just two days before my sister was abducted, the tooth fairy came, because she lost one of her back teeth. He cased the joint, Scully...

AGENT SCULLY: Mulder, I...

AGENT MULDER: Fairy, Scully. You remember your fairy tales? Little men. Foundlings? Fairy babies? Human children stolen away and taken to Fairyland? Abductions, Scully, abductions....

AGENT SCULLY: God, help me, Mulder - you're almost making some sense. But...the tooth fairy? He was probably your dad, Mulder...

AGENT MULDER: I thought my dad was Santa Claus...God, he had his secrets.

BANG!

AGENT MULDER: Owww!

AGENT SCULLY: Mulder...oh, forget it. Before you knock your teeth out, why don't you check with Skinner first to see if he'll authorise the use of a surveillance team...on the tooth fairy?

ASSISTANT DIRECTOR SKINNER: Let me get this straight. You want me to authorise a full stakeout on a pillow in your bedroom, so you can lure the tooth fairy...

AGENT MULDER: Yes, sir.

ASSISTANT DIRECTOR SKINNER: Request denied. Go home and lie down until you feel better. That's my final word. Oh, before you go Agent Mulder, I need to have a word with you about your expenses.

AGENT MULDER: Yes sir.

ASSISTANT DIRECTOR SKINNER: Four and a half million dollars?

AGENT MULDER: Yes sir.

ASSISTANT DIRERCTOR SKINNER: In the last six calendar months?

AGENT MULDER: Yes sir.

ASSISTANT DIRECTOR SKINNER: That's a lot of money, Agent Mulder.

AGENT MULDER: It's my sister, Samantha, sir. You know she was...abducted...when I was a kid. I've...evidence...to suppose she's alive and I've been hunting down her and her kidnappers.

ASSISTANT DIRECTOR SKINNER: And where's your evidence, Agent Mulder?

AGENT MULDER: She's...somehow getting these postcards to me, sir...

(Faking the following pieces of evidence took a considerable amount of time. Faking human writing is difficult and strange. For a start, they write with their hands. Incredible as it may seem, their knees play no part in it. When I say they 'write with their hands', I do not mean that they literally 'write' with their hands. They are not capable of producing ink from their fingertips - unlike the Squid Men of Aquaterra VII. They use writing instruments called 'ballpoints'. Again, this does not mean they enjoy anything in common with the Conadians of the Magellan Cluster. Thankfully.)

Dear Fox,
How are you? I hope you are fine. I am not fine. I have been kidnapped by Spacemen. I'm not sure where I am, but I think it's called Timbucktoo. Please come rescue me.

Samantha A. Mulder x

Fox Mulder
The FBI
Washington DC
America.

Dear Fox,
How are you. I hope you are fine. I am not fine because I have been stolen by naughty space boys who are not gray with big eyes because they don't exist. They say I can go if you come to the Arctic Circle and wait for me, then we can play.
love Samantha x

P.S. wear wooly socks and a scarf.

Fox Mulder
The FBI
Washington DC
America

Dear Fox,
Are you well? I am not well because I am doing experiments with the flying saucer men which means they flick rubber bands at me all day and I don't like it and the backs of my legs hurt. Please come & save me. I am in a cave somewhere in Australia.
love Samantha x

P.S. Sorry about the Arctic Circle. I meant 'Antarctica'.

Fox Mulder
The FBI
Washington DC
America

Dear Fox, how are you? I am not well because the big blue space people are trying to turn me into a shrew-girl. It turns out that I I am not in Australia but Austria - which is somewhere else. Please come for me. I think you are grown up but I am still little. So I can recognise you, come to Austria naked (there are no naked men in Austria). Love Samantha X

Fox Mulder
The FBI
Washington DC
America

Dear Fox, I saw you several times when you were in Austria but I could not get away from the bad spacemen. I am sorry you got arrested by Austrian police on indecency charges & deported. The spacemen are going to move me to the bottom of the ocean. I like dolphins. Do you? Can you steal a nuclear submarine and rescue me?
Love, Samantha X

United Nations   3c
TO UNITE OUR STRENGTH

Fox Mulder
The FBI
Washington DC
America.

Dear Fox. I am sorry you were shot by navy police & had to go to hospital. You didn't need to be naked when you tried to steal the submarine - I now know what you look like so you can wear clothes. We didn't go to the bottom of the sea after all - instead we went to outer Mongolia. I like it here. Please rescue me. The spacemen say they will make me marry the Yeti. Love Samantha X

MONGOLIA
LONDON
МОНГОЛ ШУУДАН   15c

Fox Mulder
The FBI
Washington
America.

Dear Fox. The day after I
said I was In Outer Mongolia
they took me in their
flying saucer to their big
space stations which floats
round the earth.
Can you hide away on
the Space Shuttle and
come and rescue me.
love
Samantha X

Fox Mulder
The FBI
Washington DC
America.

Dear Fox, You are silly!
Imagine stowing away on
the Space Shuttle that
was docking with the
Soyez Space Station and
having to stay up there
for 6 months. I saw you
on the TV talking about
vomiting in zero gravity
for 6 months non-stop.
Gross! I hope you are
better now.
love Samantha
X

Fox Mulder
The FBI
Washington DC
America

AGENT SCULLY

Unlike Agent Mulder, FBI Agent Dana Scully is a natural cynic. It was therefore considerably more difficult to confuse and manipulate her because of her lack of belief in the paranormal.

However, although she displayed a calm, unemotional exterior, Dana Scully proved to be quite a sensitive individual and, as such, left herself open to the exploitation of her three main insecurities:

a) Her weight
b) Her height
c) Rejection by Agent Mulder.

The success of an X-File investigation could seriously be hampered when Agent Scully suffered anxiety and uncertainty over any or all of these issues.

We found that the best way to make her paranoid about the first two was by leaving simple, anonymous messages on her home answering machine:

METHOD 1: MAKE SCULLY UNCOMFORTABLE ABOUT HER

PERSONAL APPEARANCE

℗ BLEEP! ℗

'Miss Scully, this is the North Georgetown University Hospital. We've just found your records. It seems you were admitted for intensive liposuction and not as the result of an alien abduction. That's why you remember things being done to your stomach...'

℗ BLEEP! ℗

'Scully. It's time you had a nickname like "Deep Throat" or "The Cigarette Smoking Man". How about "Munchkin"?'

℗ BLEEP! ℗

'Agent Scully, you know that man who stole your blood sample while you were in the coma, well he worked for a major chemical conglomerate which was trying to synthesise artificial pig fat.'

℗ BLEEP! ℗

'Scully, is it true that inhaling near the Cigarette Smoking Man stunted your growth?'

℗ BLEEP! ℗

'Dana, I'm trying to start a branch of Weightwatchers in the Bureau and your name was given to me by 2,563 agents as someone who might like to join.'

℗ BLEEP! ℗

'Agent Scully, I'm a NASA scientist you met during the Space Shuttle investigation. We need to create an artificial eclipse of the sun and wonder if we could borrow you for a few hours next Monday?'

'Hello beautiful. You slim, svelte, sylph-like size 8, you. Ooops! Sorry Scully, I've dialled your number by mistake.'

© BLEEP! *©*

'Dana, it's a pity that you weren't eaten by Mr Chaco in your investigation of his chicken processing plant in Arkansas. He and his conspirators could have lived off you for weeks.'

© BLEEP! *©*

'Agent Scully, Fox told me the other day that he'd rather become buddies with Krycek than go out with anyone under five feet four.'

© BLEEP! *©*

'Scully, this is Human Resources. Can you refrain from wearing high heeled-shoes to the office? Every time you walk you strike oil.'

© BLEEP! *©*

'Dana. It's me, your father, with a message from The Other Side... You're shorter than I remembered. And have you put on weight?'

© BLEEP! *©*

'Scully, I bet you were really jealous of Eugene Tooms, what with him being able to squeeze through the smallest of spaces when you have trouble getting through your office doorway.'

© BLEEP! *©*

'Special Agent Scully, I hear that the only reason you joined Mulder was because you thought you might end up investigating X-Files like the "Zero-Calorie Chocolate Cup Cakes" or "The Height Serum"?'

© BLEEP! *©*

'Scully, when you investigated those animal abductions from a zoo in Idaho I heard that Mulder saw an elephant running down the road and, until it got within twenty feet, he was convinced it was you.'

© BLEEP! *©*

'Agent Scully, we've discovered what's going on at Area 51. The Government is using reverse engineering to create a stealth corset - just for you!'

© BLEEP! *©*

'Dana, the Bureau Drama Society is putting on a performance of Snow White and we've pencilled you in for a leading role. All we need now is to find the other six dwarfs.'

© BLEEP! *©*

'Dana, Weightwatchers have asked if they can take your photograph. They want to run off a load of copies that members can stick on their fridge doors.'

© BLEEP! *©*

'Scully, Mulder's known by his colleagues as "Spooky". Is it true that you're called "Shorty" or "Podgy"?'

© BLEEP! *©*

'Agent Scully. I've just read your thesis, "Einstein's Twin Paradox: A New Interpretation" and I just wanted to say you're overweight...'

© BLEEP! *©*

'Dana, this is the Sweethearts computer dating agency: we've finally found a match for you...Detroit.'

© BLEEP! *©*

'Dana, you remember that case where people in Pennsylvania followed killing instructions on digital readouts, well is it true that when you stood on your bathroom scale the message appeared "One At A Time, Please"?'

© BLEEP! *©*

'Hi Dana. Long time no speak. The last time I saw you was at the St Patrick's Day Parade when you had ropes attached.'

1. We infiltrated her apartment, removed all the labels in her clothes and replaced them with these:

2. We replaced all her mirrors with the ones from fairgrounds so that she looked to have gained 70lb overnight. (We also rigged up an ultrasonic sound device linked to a motion sensor so that, every time the unfortunate woman approached one of the mirrors, it appeared to crack spontaneously.)

3. We fixed her bathroom scales so they were inaccurate by in excess of 14lbs.

4. Our Special Operations Unit (Ladies Wear) took in all her clothes by two inches, and weakened the seams.

5. Our Special Operations Unit (Footwear and Accessories) replaced her shoes with identical ones, one size too small.

6. On the eve of a vital investigation we completely undermined Scully by launching a new glossy upmarket magazine (circulation 400,000) backed up by a nationwide TV campaign, just so that she could find this on her local newsstand (and every other newsstand in the country)...

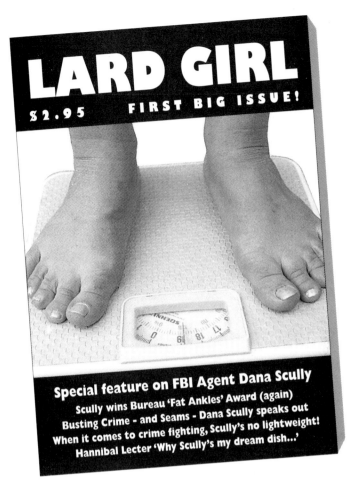

METHOD 3: CONVINCE SCULLY THAT SHE IS EVEN SHORTER THAN SHE THINKS SHE IS (AND SHRINKING)...

1. Our Special Operations Unit (Joinery and Tiling) lowered the floor in her apartment by 2". This might seem drastic, however, the effect of her discovering she couldn't quite reach shelving etc. was well worth the effort.

2. The same unit then lowered the floor in her apartment by 12", forcing her to get up on a chair to reach the work surfaces.

3. To further confound her, we raised light switches, the wash basin, shelving, shower head and every mirror in the apartment.

4. Finally, we removed all her furniture and replaced it with exact replicas that were 1.5 times larger.

METHOD 4: CONVINCE SCULLY THAT SHE HAS SERIOUS RIVALS FOR

FOX MULDER'S ATTENTION

Although playing on her fears of being overweight and under height was effective in hampering her efficiency, we found that the best method of inducing serious psychological torment undoubtedly came from making her believe that Agent Mulder hated her - or even better - was having an affair with one or more bimbos - a kind of woman she particularly despises, but whom, by all account, Agent Mulder was rather taken by.

We crafted letters such as these and arranged to have them dropped in her internal post and through her apartment letterbox.

Dana,

I thought I'd better let you know that Mulder organises call girls for Senator Matheson and they spent last weekend holed up in the Washington Hilton with three babes apiece and a bucket of whipped cream.

X

A tall friend.

Scully,

While you were in a coma, Mulder slept with 182 different women including your sister. And your mum.

Another tall friend.

Dear Dana,

You don't know me but when you see that hunky partner of yours, Fox, tell him that he left his boxer shorts in my apartment last night

Tania.

Tania (5' 8 1/2")

Dana,

You weren't around to investigate the vampire cult so I was able to sleep with Fox. He's OK though. His blood was the one thing I didn't suck...

K

Kristen (6'1")

Dear Dana,
I just wanted to tell you to get your mitts off Fox. He's mine! I might not be as clever as you but I've got a 48 DD bust and I'm double-jointed and my legs are taller than you are!

Boozie

Ps And I'm 5'9" (without my 4" red leather stilettoes), you little buttsniffer!

Dear Dana,

Do you remember me? I was at Oxford with Fox and met you recently when I got involved with that case involving Cecil L'ively, the firestarter.

All I wanted to say was that after meeting you I know I've got no competition.

Love,

Phoebe

Phoebe Green (5'8")

Dana,
wen you see Fox, tell him that i had the tests and im not pregnant. This is grate news as it meens i can carry on my carear as a lap-danser.
Luv,
Roxanne   (6' - and awl leg!)

Dear Dana,
You don't know me but when you see that ranky partner of yours, Fox, tell him he left his boxer shorts in my apartment last night.

Larry   (8½")
x

Dana,
Did you know that Fox also calls me "Deep Throat"...
Love Tiffany. (above average height!).
XXXX.

While Mulder was usually the believer and Scully the sceptic, the position was reversed when it came to religious beliefs. Scully was born and raised a Catholic, which is a kind of religion, and so harbours strange religious beliefs which were ripe for exploitation - unlike her partner, who was fiercely atheistic.

With this in mind, we initiated religious based hoaxes to draw Agent Scully away from our trail...

FBI MEMO SHEET

F.B.I.

FROM: Mulder,

TO:

DATE:

Don't come near me! I saw those three sixes on the back of your neck! You're the anti-christ! The devil's whelp! I don't want my eyes pecked out by ravens or get cut in half in an elevator or fall under the ice! I hereby resign from the X-Files and I shall spend the rest of my life in a nunnery. To think I ~~══════════~~

Scully

P.S. I am not hiding in the big stationery cupboard in our office. No way. That would be much too obvious.

Scully,
I am pushing this note under the cupboard door now. I am not the anti-christ. The 666s were written on the back of my neck in ball point. Must have happened when I fell asleep. I am only moderately evil. Friends again?
M.

I'm not in here!
S.

My years of FBI training tell me you are, Scully.
M.

Whore of Babylon!
S.

I'm male. How can I be a whore of anything?
M.

I don't know. Rent Boy of Babylon then!
S.

Wait while I go and Xerox the back of my neck.
M.

am working on this X-File by myself, because of Agent Mulder's conviction that it is a steaming pile of the horse proverbial'.

Mulder knows nothing about religion. He thinks the Primate of All Ireland is a distant relative of Bigfoot. He thinks Confession is some kind of new TV game show. He thinks catechism is something like what happened at Three Mile Island or Chernobyl. Ha ha.

To think, what I am holding in my hand could be the very foreskin of John the Baptist. (Well, not actually in my hand. That would be disgusting. In a small petri dish in my hand.)

A Christian Fundamentalist was caught at La Guardia airport, trying to smuggle it in disguised as a wedding ring. Under questioning, he admitted it had been stolen from the Vatican, and some kind of potato chip called a *Hula-Hoop* left in its place.

He said that Christian scientists planned to clone John the Baptist back from his earthly remains, as harbinger to 'the Second Coming'. My mind races at such an audacious plan! Do I smell fraud? No, I checked, it's the specimen.

This could be the most important X-File of all time! If only Mulder wasn't too down on religion to think clearly!

Anyway, tomorrow, the specimen goes to the FBI labs. DNA and RNA testing should determine at least the racial grouping of the specimen, while carbon testing and other trace element-based tests might give us a better clue as to the sample's actual age and help determine if it is genuine...

There's no time to send the specimen off to the labs tonight, so I'll leave it in the office until first thing tomorrow. I don't care how long this operation takes, or how many months I must spend on it. If there is a move to clone John the Baptist to act once more as a herald, this could be important physical evidence that the End Times are upon us.

One tiny specimen. It could mean so much...

Scully,
Thanks for leaving me your last Hula-Hoop
I didn't know you cared.
Anyway, it hit the spot. I haven't
had a Hula-Hoop since I was at Oxford
with Phoebe.
I'm at the Congress Library now until
lunchtime, if you need me.

Mulder.

TRANSCRIPT FROM NSA SURVEILLANCE
APARTMENT OF SPECIAL AGENT DANA KATHERINE SCULLY, MD. 3170 W. 53 Rd.
#35, Annapolis, MD.

DOOR KNOCKING SOUND

AGENT MULDER: Sorry I'm late, Scully. There was a triple homicide just around the corner. Three winos were found with their skulls opened and their brains missing...

MUFFLED VOICE: Brains...

AGENT MULDER: Melissa? Melissa Scully?

AGENT SCULLY: This is the surprise I mentioned on the phone. Isn't it wonderful? Somehow she's alive...

MELISSA SCULLY: Brains!

AGENT MULDER: [WHISPERED] Scully, her nose is missing...

AGENT SCULLY: Please...don't mention it. Or the...you know...smell. She's obviously been through a lot and can't bring herself to talk about it... Just act like nothing is wrong. Take that handkerchief away from over your face for a start!

AGENT MULDER: What's she wearing? Chanel Roadkill Number 5?

AGENT SCULLY: I...I thought we'd all go out to dinner - to celebrate Melissa's return to us. I...I've invited Assistant Director Skinner as Melissa's date.

AGENT MULDER: You did what?

MELISSA SCULLY: Brains! Brains! Brains! Brains! Brains! Brains!

SURVEILLANCE
PHOTOGRAPH:
MELISSA SCULLY.

AGENT MULDER: Scully...I don't want to say anything - but I think Melissa left her foot in the car...

AGENT SCULLY: Shhhh! Here's Skinner.

ASSISTANT DIRECTOR SKINNER: Mulder. Scully. Melissa! You're looking...er...very well, Melissa.

AGENT MULDER: For someone with no feet and no nose.

AGENT SCULLY: Mulder! Melissa, Assistant Director Skinner here risked his life for you when we...thought...you'd been killed. He insisted on continuing to investigate your...death...even when he was told not...

MELISSA SCULLY: Brains!

AGENT MULDER: I liked her better when she whittered on about magic crystals and horoscopes...

ASSISTANT DIRECTOR SKINNER: Hey, Melissa, look. I like you but...you know. Could you...do you think you could...stop licking my head?

MELISSA SCULLY: Brains...

AGENT SCULLY: She's always gone for smart men, sir...

ASSISTANT DIRECTOR SKINNER: Oww! She bit my head!

MELISSA SCULLY: BRAINS!

VIOLENT SCUFFLING NOISES

AGENT MULDER: She's a zombie, Scully! Get back!

ASSISTANT DIRECTOR SKINNER: Get her off me! She's trying to bite my scalp off!

VIOLENT SCUFFLING NOISES

AGENT SCULLY: Er...Melissa. Can you stop that, please?

AGENT MULDER: You can't reason with it, Scully! It's dead! I've got to blow its brain out!

VIOLENT SCUFFLING NOISES

ASSISTANT DIRECTOR SKINNER: Ahhh! Don't bite my ear off. How am I gonna keep my glasses on?

MELISSA SCULLY: BRAINS!

AGENT SCULLY: We must take her alive!

AGENT MULDER: She's a zombie....That's going to be difficult...

AGENT SCULLY: Mulder, no!!!!!!!!

BLAM-BLAM-BLAM-BLAM-BLAM-BLAM-BLAM-BLAM!

AGENT SCULLY: Let me help you up sir, oh dear, you're bleeding. I'm so sorry. I never thought my sister would try to eat your brains...

ASSISTANT DIRECTOR SKINNER: You got any more relatives you want to fix me up with, Agent Scully?

WAITER: Erm...excuse me...is there an Agent Mulder here?

AGENT MULDER: That's me.

WAITER: Phone call for you, Agent Mulder. From your father...

LOVE

It seemed a simple enough plan: we would make Agents Mulder and Scully fall in love and become so wrapped up in each other that they would lose all interest in what we were doing.

The problem came when we tried to understand the human notion of 'love'. What is it? Your guess is as good as mine. Love, whatever it is, only seems to exist on this planet. In all the known worlds, it has never been encountered before.

To add to our problems, even humans do not seem to agree on what this thing is. They sing about it frequently, but their messages and theories are highly contradictory and - it seems - rather unreliable.

We listened to all their most popular notions about love, and then despatched Special Operations Teams to investigate further.

Their results were...rather disappointing:

Team 8 were sent out to discover whether or not love was caused by extreme violence. Our first clue that this might have been so came from the songstress Pat Benetar who suggested that 'Love is A Battlefield'. Many seemed to agree with her, including Jim Capaldi who said that 'Love Hurts' and Alice Cooper who, rather bizarrely, thought that 'Love's A Loaded Gun'. More investigation is needed, if only to eliminate this curious theory.

Team 9, working from the notion of the wise human John Paul Young that 'Love is in the Air', completed a full range of diagnostics on the planetary atmosphere. No single component could be identified that could be linked to 'the love phenomenon'. Further investigations were proposed into the effects of localised electro-magnetic fields.

Team 10 had been sent in search of 'The Love Machine'. No record of any such machine existed in the patents office, they reported. Investigations are continuing, as many songs refer to 'making love' and we can only assume that this is the machine that makes it...

Team 11 had spent several weeks in search of 'The Love Train' sung about by The O Jays. Despite having some very useful clues such as 'Our first stop will be England' and knowing that the train made stops in Africa,

Egypt, Israel, Russia and China too, they were completely unable to locate any such route being operated by any train company. They thought that the train might now have gone out of service.

Team 12 reported that, despite completing a detailed geophysical mapping of every country on the planet, they had not discovered anywhere called 'Love Town' and had drawn a complete blank on locating 'The Love Shack', and its mysterious occupant 'The Loveshack Baby'...

Team 13, which had been asked to further examine the proposition that 'Love Makes the World Go Around', reported that, if this was true, there had to be some kind of connection between love and the rotation of a spherical body relative to its polar axis, strongly suggesting that gravity and motion might have a part to play. This was backed up by the assertion that 'Love Is All Around' because, if the former statement were true, love would appear to be all around to someone standing on the surface of the revolving sphere. If love were related to the centrifugal motion of bodies, they suggested that whirling people around might produce a short-lasting experience similar to love. This was possibly how the 'Love Machine' worked.

Team 14 had been assigned to follow the lead 'Love Grows Where My Rosemary Goes'. They reported that there are approximately 470,000 Rosemarys in the world, and a further 170,000 Rose Maries or derivations thereof. It was impossible to know which Rosemary was being referred to. It was also impossible to watch all of them for signs of unusual plant growth or other love-related activity subsequent to their passing. The biological mechanism by which Love grew relative to the movement of the individual could not therefore be ascertained.

Team 15, who had been assigned to discover if there was any truth in the assertion that 'Love is the Drug' reported that 'Green lobsters lived between the diamond bushes'.

Team 16, who had been assigned the lead 'Love Me, Love My Dog' and the possibly rhetorical 'Ain't Love A Bitch?' reported in sick.

Team 17 had completely failed to locate the sub-species of feline known as 'The Love Cats'.

As the great philosopher Alexander O'Neal said, 'Love makes no sense'...

We then decided to fall back on that useful stand-by - carnal attraction. However, once again, we were baffled as to how to bring Agents Mulder and Scully together. What could they possibly find attractive about each other, being large, hairy, small eyed and pink skinned? We have long found human beings physically repulsive - which is why the biggest sex symbol and only turn on for us on the whole planet is Smurfette - and cannot begin to comprehend their mating requirements.

Even their physical mating act is strange. Parts of the body you would normally expect to be involved - such as the kneecaps and nasal pasages - are almost completely ignored!

We fell back on the most similar species known to us - the Centauris - but discovered that although the two species were very alike, they had very distinct mating rituals...

TRANSCRIPT FROM NSA SURVEILLANCE OPERATION:
LOCATION: BASEMENT, FBI BUILDING

AGENT SCULLY: What's this parcel for me?

AGENT MULDER: Maybe you got a secret admirer, Scully...

AGENT SCULLY: I wish. Can I borrow your knife?

AGENT MULDER: Sure.

AGENT SCULLY: Thanks...I...oh! Oh my God! Oh! Oh! I'm going to be sick!

AGENT MULDER: I guess it's not from the book club then...

Similar species. Very different rituals. Unlike the Centauri, apparently humans do not send each other their spoor in gift packets.

Likewise, impromptu all-night performances of the finest Centauri love yodels outside Scully's apartment also failed to make any impression upon her hormonal drive.

Further tests failed to get anything but a negative response from other Centauri mating traditions. Genital imprints, urine soaked socks, dead rodents in aspic, squashed insects pressed onto card in the shape of a diamond - nothing worked.

Then one of our biochemists made a significant discovery. He looked at the symptoms humans reported when they were in love - increased pulse rate, sweating, mild delirium, upset stomach, trembling and shaking - and concluded that love must be caused by Salmonella bacteria. Brilliant. Of course, a bacteriological agent. Love wasn't the drug - it was the bug!

We put our plan into action immediately, and arranged to have the agents flown to Paris on a special mission...

TRANSCRIPT FROM NSA SURVEILLANCE OPERATION:
LOCATION: AIR FRANCE BOEING 747 F-FDGH.

AGENT MULDER: What's this?

STEWARDESS: A whole finest Grade A American chicken for your dinner, monsieur...and for you mademoiselle.

AGENT MULDER: We're not getting the cold burger and congealed gravy like everyone else?

AGENT SCULLY: Don't look a gift horse in the mouth, Mulder. Eat up!

The bacteriological agent having been installed, we then set up a massive surveillance operation and gathered around to watch the consummation of our plans...

What had seemed so promising turned out to be a dismal failure.

AGENT SCULLY: I don't believe it. They mixed up our reservation. They only had the bridal suite. Can you believe it?

AGENT MULDER: Don't worry. I'll take the bath, Scully...Your virtue is safe. Have you ever been to Paris before?

AGENT SCULLY: No.

AGENT MULDER: It's fabulous. Why don't we take a walk, maybe have a meal, some drinks, see the sights. Just soak up the city, then catch a late show together...

AGENT SCULLY: Careful Mulder, you almost sound romantic...

AGENT MULDER: That's Paris for you. Look, I just have to go to the bathroom first...

(45 minutes later)

AGENT SCULLY: Mulder, are you feeling OK?

AGENT MULDER: [MUFFLED] God, Scully, give me my gun. Let me end it quickly...bleuggghh!

AGENT SCULLY: Er...Mulder. I think I might have to use the bathroom...

AGENT MULDER: [MUFFLED] Not a chance, Scully...oh God...oh...oh...

(45 minutes later)

AGENT SCULLY: Let me in you selfish bastard! I'm dying...oh...bleurrgh!

AGENT MULDER: [MUFFLED] I think I just brought up my pancreas, Scully...

AGENT SCULLY: Mulder...whatever you do...don't look in your suitcase when you get out here...

AGENT MULDER: [MUFFLED] You're the doctor, Scully. Do something!

AGENT SCULLY: I can't...I can't move...

AGENT MULDER: [MUFFLED] Oh...that was intestine. That was definitely intestine...

AGENT SCULLY: Shut up, Mulder! You're making me feel...bleuurrgh! I, I hope you brought another raincoat with you...

We had one gambit left. There were strong rumours among humans that love made them feel young again. Could the reverse also be true? If we were to make Mulder and Scully feel young again, would they fall in love? Chemicals were introduced via their apartments' separate water supplies and we waited for them to take effect...

TRANSCRIPT FROM NSA SURVEILLANCE OPERATION:
LOCATION: BASEMENT, FBI BUILDING

AGENT MULDER: Hey Scully. You wanna play D & D with me? Dungeons and Dragons? It's really cool!

AGENT SCULLY: You are such a dork, Mulder! Puhlease!

AGENT MULDER: Aw, come on Scully, you can be an Orc. They're pretty good! And you can have plus three for strength and a plus four for stamina...

AGENT SCULLY: Get lost, Moldy! That's for kids! Here, wanna have a swig of this?

AGENT MULDER: That's alcohol!

AGENT SCULLY: Sure is.

AGENT MULDER: I'm gonna tell on you, Scully! You are in soooo much trouble...

AGENT SCULLY: Like I'm afraid of old Skinhead. Like, puhlease!

ASSISTANT DIRECTOR SKINNER: Good morning Scully, Mulder...

AGENT SCULLY: Ulp...

AGENT MULDER: Principal Skinner, sir. Scully's got alcohol and she's been drinking, sir.

AGENT SCULLY: Sneak!

ASSISTANT DIRECTOR SKINNER: What's with you two this morning?

AGENT MULDER: It's not me sir, it's her, sir.

AGENT SCULLY: Wimp!

ASSISTANT DIRECTOR SKINNER: I'll come back later.

AGENT SCULLY: You are soooo dead, Mulder!

AGENT MULDER: You hurt me and I'll tell!

AGENT SCULLY: Shut up or I'll twist your stupid ear off, you little virgin.

AGENT MULDER: I am not!

AGENT SCULLY: Yeah? And who'd let you? Do me a favour!

AGENT MULDER: Er...do you want to go out with me this Friday?

AGENT SCULLY: I wouldn't go out with you if you were Donny Osmond himself!

Another failure. We recognise that love is totally incomprehensible to us and we abandoned all attempts to bring the two agents together, accepting that Mulder and Scully would remain wedded to their jobs.

ABDUCTIONS

Disinformation.

It's one of the most important weapons in our arsenal.

It's even more important than the heat ray (although you don't feel nearly so masculine and empowered and - let's be honest - *tall* spreading disinformation as you do when it's your turn to sit in the turret and practise operating the heat ray).

When you're operating hundreds of thousands of flights in Earth air space each year, as we do, it's inevitable that we're going to be seen, by witnesses on the ground, by pilots and by earth radar.

Abductees, too, may remember being snatched by us. Screen memories and the amnesio-serum are only so effective and it is inevitable that some proportion of the Large Ones we snatch will recall the experience.

Our disinformation operations are vital. We must make the subject of UFOs a joke, so that no one can take witnesses seriously.

To achieve this, we have been employing two distinctly different techniques with which you need to be familiar...

METHOD 1: MANIPULATION OF EARTH MEDIA

We enjoy excellent relations with the human entrepreneurs called 'press barons'. Long skilled at manipulating public opinion for their own gain, they have been only too willing to help ridicule the UFO phenomenon, in return for small favours such as aerial photographs of celebrity weddings.

Here, typically, is how UFO reports are manipulated in the press:

HUMANS SAY...
MYSTERIOUS LIGHTS FOLLOWED MY CAR

OUR AGENTS PRINT...

I HUMPED 4ODD SPACE BIMBETTE IN STAR SLIME JACUZZI

HUMANS SAY...
'GRAY MEN' ABDUCTED
ME CLAIMS CIRCUIT JUDGE

OUR AGENTS PRINT...

SPACE BEAVERS BUILT DAM UP MY NOSE SAYS TOWN DRUNK

HUMANS SAY...
LANDED SAUCER LEAVES MARKS ON
GROUND

OUR AGENTS PRINT...

JIM CARREY IS ET, CLAIMS SEX CHANGE MERMAID HUNTER

HUMANS SAY...
F-16 PILOT IN AERIAL 'NEAR MISS'
WITH UFO

OUR AGENTS PRINT...

...terstellar hot-rodders drag race US air space, says witness

HUMANS SAY...
CIGAR SHAPED OBJECT DOES
MACH 10 OVER OHIO

OUR AGENTS PRINT...

WE MURDERED NICOLE, CLAIMS NEW ET OJ WITNESS

HUMANS SAY...
200 PEOPLE SEE
UFO OVER
WASHINGTON DC

**OUR AGENTS
PRINT...**

Barbra to wed Loch Ness monster... says agent

HUMANS SAY...
ALIEN 'MEDICAL
EXAM' LEAVES
SCARS ON
WITNESS

**OUR AGENTS
PRINT...**

Aliens taught me secret of better dieting - delicious intergalactic seven day diet plan inside!

HUMANS SAY...
AIR FORCE BAFFLED BY UFO 'WAVE'

OUR AGENTS PRINT...

AIR FORCE SAY UFO WITNESSES ARE 'ASSHOLES' - IT'S OFFICIAL

HUMANS SAY...
UFO FORCES CAR OFF INTERSTATE

OUR AGENTS PRINT...

CHER HAS BIGFOOT'S LOVE CHILD

HUMANS SAY...
RADIATION TRACES FOUND AFTER
'CLOSE ENCOUNTER'

OUR AGENTS PRINT...

Bruce and Demi to split - OFFICIAL

HUMANS SAY...
ETs STOLE MY UNBORN BABY

OUR AGENTS PRINT...

ETs STOLE MY UNBORN BABY

Decorate your craft with a slogan. No one will believe a witness who reports a 'saucer' decorated like the examples below...

(They'll certainly never believe that one...)

We know too, that by behaving in unusual ways with abductees, we can discredit their accounts totally. Agents Mulder and Scully were thrown completely off our trail by - if you'll excuse the language - the *tall* tales witnesses recounted to them...

DETAIL FROM J/338923/34. Interview conducted by Agent Scully 07/03/96

WITNESS J: They said they came from...from...

AGENT SCULLY: Yes?

WITNESS J: They said they came from the planet...Penis.

AGENT SCULLY: Well, thank you, sir. Thank you for talking to us. We'll be in touch if we can take this any further...

WITNESS J: 5000 light years away in the constellation of Wobblybottom...

AGENT SCULLY: Oh, I think I can hear someone calling my name...I've got to go now. Please see yourself out.

DETAIL FROM X/276423/64. Interview conducted by Agent Mulder 06/17/96

WITNESS X: And...and then they forced to me drink lots of fifteen-year-old malt whisky and I don't remember anything more until the Highway Patrol stopped me doing 110 down the wrong side of I-90. You...you do believe what I'm saying, don't you?

AGENT MULDER: How do I put this?...ah...Not a word.

DETAIL FROM K/296523/37. Interview conducted by Agent Mulder 06/23/96

WITNESS K: After they'd extracted the sperm sample, they took me on a tour of the ship. The strangest thing was...there were posters of Jon Bon Jovi absolutely every place I looked...and Motley Crue.

AGENT MULDER: Are you sure you were in a space ship? Is it possible you were somewhere else...like in a record store perhaps?

WITNESS K: Since when does Tower Records remove your semen, Agent Mulder?

AGENT MULDER: It beats 'Any 3 CDs for $30' offers, I'll give you that...

DETAIL FROM C/346463/74. Interview conducted by Agent Scully 07/01/96

WITNESS C: After...after...oh God, it's so awful you'll never understand...

AGENT SCULLY: It's OK. I...I may have been abducted too. I do understand what you're going through. Carry on...Please.

WITNESS C: Afterwards they...they showed me the future...scenes of the Earth being attacked and destroyed. They...they said only I could stop it. One of them got out a board game - Ker-Plunk!!, I think it was called, and they challenged me to a game. If I lost, the Earth would be destroyed, they said. Did that happen to you too, Agent Scully?

AGENT SCULLY: (LOUD COUGHING) No, no it didn't...

DETAIL FROM E/192433/65. Interview conducted by Agent Mulder 06/17/96

WITNESS E: I was strapped on this table. This gray figure was looming right over me. I said, 'who are you?' And...and this telepathic message formed in my brain. 'Call me...Dave...'

AGENT MULDER: Go home.

DETAIL FROM P/133453/54. Interview conducted by Agent Mulder 06/23/96

WITNESS P: And then I received this...overwhelming...telepathic message. It said 'beware he who calls himself...Tony the Tiger...'

DETAIL FROM L/491423/33. Interview conducted by Agent Scully 06/17/96

WITNESS L: They said...they said they had come to Earth to get...dancing lessons...

AGENT SCULLY: Do you have any strong medication in your house?

WITNESS L: Earth is the only place you can learn the Charleston, they said...

AGENT SCULLY: Barbituates? Hallucinogens? Solvents? Crack cocaine?

WITNESS L: As I watched, two of these small gray creatures started to...started to foxtrot together. Right there, right in front of me.

AGENT SCULLY: I'm afraid I'm going to have to ask you to come with me, sir...

WITNESS L: Why? Where are you taking me?

AGENT SCULLY: The nearest side door I can eject you from...

DETAIL FROM I/356663/31. Interview conducted by Agents Mulder and Scully 06/14/96

WITNESS I: I was left strapped to the table, but the paralysis was wearing off. I managed to turn my head to the left and...and...I can't explain this...at all. I saw President Clinton, strapped down on the table next to me. And he was...OK, OK, he was wearing a dress.

AGENT SCULLY: The President of the United States? In a dress. Thank you. I think that's all we need for now.

AGENT MULDER: Wait Scully. (TO WITNESS) Did he say anything about a transvesti ray? Think! Try to remember! It's important!

AGENT SCULLY: Mulder...

WITNESS I: No, nothing about a 'transvestite ray', but then this 'Gray' came back a he said 'Now we want you and the President of the United States to mate' and I remember thinking, 'No - I'm a married man!'

AGENT MULDER: OK, Scully, get him out of here...

DETAIL FROM N/338469/04. Interview conducted by Agent Scully 06/17/96

AGENT SCULLY: I'm sorry, ma'am, but I'm going to have to end this now. The FBI closes early on a Thursday.

WITNESS N: But they did...they did put a custard pie in my face! Why won't you believe me?

DETAIL FROM Z/126433/25. Interview conducted by Agent Mulder 06/21/96

WITNESS Z: They did! They stood there and did this a cappella number, all four of them...

DETAIL FROM N/278923/35. Interview conducted by Agent Mulder 07/11/96

WITNESS N: So there I was. It was about 9pm. I'd just finished my television evangelist show...

AGENT MULDER: Next!

DETAIL FROM F/267893/53. Interview conducted by Agent Mulder 07/01/96

WITNESS F: They want our socks! That's what they said. That's why we keep ending up with only half a pair. Oh God, why won't anyone believe me! They're here! No hosiery is safe! Your socks are next! Keep watching the drawers!

DETAIL FROM Q/356723/38. Interview conducted by Agent Scully 06/30/96

WITNESS Q: They said they came from the planet (LOUD RASPING SOUND).

AGENT SCULLY: The planet (LOUD RASPING SOUND)?

WITNESS Q: In the galaxy of (THREE LOUD RASPS, TWO SQUEAKS AND A CLUCKING NOISE).

AGENT SCULLY: In the galaxy they call (THREE LOUD RASPS, THREE SQUEAKS AND A CLUCKING NOISE)?

WITNESS Q: No. (THREE LOUD RASPS, TWO SQUEAKS AND A CLUCKING NOISE) We must get it right. It could be important.

AGENT SCULLY: Somehow I doubt it.

WITNESS Q: They said they had a message I had to convey to the FBI.

AGENT SCULLY: And what was that?

WITNESS Q: (LOUD RASPING SOUND LASTING APPROXIMATELY TEN AND ONE HALF SECONDS)

CATTLE ABDUCTION
AND MUTILATION

Inter-breeding with the humans is our primary purpose here on this world. This is done exclusively through artificial insemination, as you could not possibly be expected to want to mate normally with something with hair and big teeth. Just think of Julia Roberts smiling up at you as you attempt sexual congress...it's a truly ghastly thought, I'm sure you'll agree.

During the first abduction, the female human is therefore impregnated artificially prior to release back into her environment. The foetus is then removed from the mother during a follow-up abduction some three months later and brought to term in a gestation tank before being 'born' and taken to the ship's nursery. Consequently, at any one time, we are likely to have up to seven hundred hybrid babies on board ship in the nursery - all of whom require regular changing, burping, feeding, bathing and comforting.

As you know, all ships come complete with a Nappy Changing Officer, but as the suicide rate among this rank is extremely high (97-99%), you may well be called upon to perform the duty by yourself. Other duties may include:

Picking up toys
Wiping crayon marks off the viewscreens, tractor beam console and diagnostic equipment
Telepathic projection of lullabies and nursery rhymes
Clearing up after synchronised bouts of 'projectile vomiting' (hybrids are half human and do not cope with 5G mid-air turns as well as we do)
Attending to crying babies (often up to three hundred at a time)
Burping and winding
Bathing
Comforting and calming of distressed halflings
Feeding
Teaching rudimentary colouring-in skills

Seven hundred hybrid babies also means seven hundred constantly hungry mouths to feed - which is, of course, why we abduct cattle. Cows' milk is an excellent free source of nutrition (and the cows themselves are an excellent source of free steaks afterwards!).

Some tips for obtaining milk from cows

1. Do not waste time looking for a ring pull, screw-off lid or vacu-seal. This is a natural biological entity.
2. Manipulate the udders as shown in your training manual.
3. Cattle abduction is done at night, from relatively high altitudes. Be very sure that the animal you have is really a cow...

This is a cow

This is a bull

Bulls do not give milk. Bulls are trouble. Bulls do not like being seized by a tractor beam and abruptly whisked several thousand feet up in the air. More than this, they do not like you trying to milk them, as this transcript of a recent tragic event over Idaho demonstrates...

EBE 1: This cow is deformed. It has but a single udder...
EBE 2: Don't touch...
BULL: Mooo!
EBE 1: Ooofff!
EBE 2: Look out!
EBE 1: Ooof!
BULL: Moooo!
EBE 1: I think we've upset it.
EBE 2: Eek!
BULL: Moo!
EBE 1: Nice cow...nice cow...
EBE 2: Oof!
BULL: Snort!
EBE 2: Let me in! Help!
EBE 1: I'm in this cupboard! You find your own hiding place!

Cattle abduction - and the milk it brings - is vital to our hybrid programme. The humans must never discover that we are behind it - or why we do it.

This is just one reason why *cults* are so useful to us. To confuse Agents Mulder and Scully about the widespread abduction of cattle from the American Mid-West, we set up a cult for gullible humans, who *claimed* they were behind the cattle rustling.

X-FILE X-78978
COMPUTER REF: OPERATION HORNY
REPORT BY AGENT FOX MULDER
EYES ONLY

Since the late 1940s, hundreds of thousands of head of cattle have mysteriously gone missing from the American prairies. Some turn up dead, with pieces missing, cut away with almost surgical precision. One school of thought suggests that UFOs might be involved. Mysterious lights are often seen in the area at the time of abductions. Another theory is that a bizarre cult is involved in snatching the cows, for purposes unknown.

Our X-File investigation began when 'X' left a newspaper at my door - a copy of the *Wyoming Advertiser*. Inside, circled, was a small box ad:

DO YOU LIKE COWS?

Really like them? Are you opposed to butter, cheese and other oppressive products of the dairy? Do you think they hold the key to the secrets of the universe? If so, you should join us.

Reply 'Cowboy' Box 614, Cheyenne, Wyoming.

Scully and I flew to Cheyenne under cover, posing as a couple of cow enthusiasts. I drafted a quick note to 'Cowboy' and we waited in our motel for a response.

Motel Six
Dry Gulch, Wyoming

Dear Cowboy,

My wife and I are really into cows. Fresian are our favourites, although we're very partial to most breeds. We'd love to join a club that's devoted to cows and to get more involved in cow-related activities generally. Please let us know more!

Ruminants rule!

Yours

Fox Mulder.

P.S. We both really hate gorgonzola and would like to see it wiped off the face of this planet!

Two days later, we were contacted by two men who looked like farmers, driving a grey sedan. They identified themselves as 'High Priests of the Brotherhood of the Bovine' and invited us to join them.

We were driven to their cult headquarters, a cattle farm between Cheyenne and Forked Butte. Here we were put through standard indoctrination techniques, albeit with a cowish-slant. We tended the cattle. We chanted 'moo' for hours on end. We were only allowed to walk around on all fours, and had bells tied around our necks.

After several mindless weeks of cow-related activity, during which we were allowed hardly any sleep or food, we were finally taken before the cult's leader - Clarabell.

Clarabell was meant to be a cosmic creature. She was, in fact, nothing more, than two men in a shoddy pantomime cow outfit. Scully spotted it immediately, and had trouble stifling her giggles. I kept a straight face.

In preparation for the forthcoming trial, I include an accurate account of the ritual that followed.

OUR LEADER - AND A VERY CLOSE FRIEND

PANTOMIME COW: I am Clarabell, cosmic cow of the Brotherhood of the Bovine.

AGENT MULDER: I am Initiate Fox Mulder and this is my wife Initiate Scully.

PANTOMIME COW: Oh. I'm sorry. We can't have anyone here called Fox. A fox isn't a ruminant. It's a canine. Completely different.

AGENT MULDER: Oh did I say Fox? I meant Bull. Bull Mulder. (*My quick thinking saves the day once again!*)

PANTOMIME COW: Welcome Bull Mulder. Welcome Initiate Scully. You seek the secrets of the cow?

AGENT MULDER: We do.

PANTOMIME COW: Is your wife *laughing*, Bull Mulder?

AGENT MULDER: Er...no, your - cowness. She has - hay fever. Which is why tears are streaming down her face...

PANTOMIME COW: Not very promising, Bull Mulder. Cows eat hay. She may not be one of us...why does she roll about on the floor like that?

AGENT MULDER: Um...she's bowing at your feet.

PANTOMIME COW: I see. So, Initiate Mulder, are you ready to receive the secret of the Bovine Brotherhood?

AGENT MULDER: We are ready to lock horns with the dilemma of cow consciousness - Scully! Stop it! Cud it out...

PANTOMIME COW: Mooooo! We cows came down from the stars aeons ago. Our planet was grazed out and we sought pastures new. We settled among you, watching, waiting, grazing as you obediently milked us, guarding you from those who would take your world from you. At night, we levitate to our cow starships to do battle with our arch enemies - the sheep.

AGENT SCULLY: The sheep? Stop it - please stop it. Oh God - I can't take any more...

PANTOMIME COW: The sheep are an ancient, evil race.

AGENT SCULLY: Haaaaaa!

PANTOMIME COW: Great are the battles. Terrible are the losses. Brave cows die, torn by sheep lasers to be discovered lifeless in the pastures the next day. They die heroes. Would you join us, humans? Would you devote all your wordly goods, charge cards and bank accounts so that we may continue to defend this world from the woolly ones?

AGENT MULDER: So, the sheep are baaaaaad guys, are they?

PANTOMIME COW: Yes.

AGENT SCULLY: Mulder, Stop it!

AGENT MULDER: How could they have pulled the wool over our eyes all these years, eh Scully?

AGENT SCULLY: I'll - get you - for this, Mulder.

PANTOMIME COW: So, are you in? We take Mastercard, Amex...

(At this point we drew our weapons and identified ourselves.)

PANTOMIME COW: Ahhh! You said your name was Bull. We trusted you!

AGENT MULDER: Stow it, Daisy!

PANTOMIME COW: This is entrapment.

AGENT MULDER: Take it up with the DA - if you've got a beef.

AGENT SCULLY: You - bastard - Mulder...

AGENT MULDER: You're going to the pen...Yippe-yi-ay! Let's round 'em up and herd 'em out, Scully...Cow Fraud...there's nothing low-er.

AGENT MULDER: You're - dead - Mulder...

It had taken weeks, but we had finally cracked the mystery of cattle abductions and mutilation. The fraudsters running the cult were fooling members into believing that our cows were engaged in interstellar war. They were killing cows to fake casualties of war. An unlikely notion to base your belief system on, perhaps, but there are millions of Buddhists...

I was disappointed not to find a connection between cattle abductions and human abductions. I guess there really isn't one. Sadly, it's all bull...

We judged this operation an outstanding success. We had wasted several weeks of Agents Mulder and Scully's time and - at the end of the day - had also successfully disguised what was really going on...

SECRET GOVERNMENT PROJECTS

Sometimes, all we needed to do to keep Mulder and Scully busy was to reveal one of their own government's secrets, then sit back, and enjoy all the trouble we'd caused everyone involved...

X-FILE X-72365

COMPUTER REF: BLACK TIES

REPORT BY AGENT FOX MULDER

EYES ONLY

I received a computer disk in the mail this morning. Anonymously. It could have come from X. It may not have done.

Wherever it came from, what was on the disk was pure dynamite - evidence of the most massive government fraud of all time...

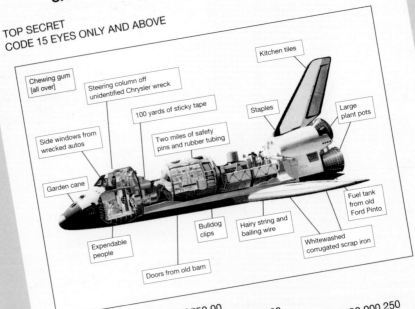

NASA
SPACE SHUTTLE DESIGN SPECIFICATIONS

TOP SECRET
CODE 15 EYES ONLY AND ABOVE

Kitchen tiles

Chewing gum [all over]

Steering column off unidentified Chrysler wreck

100 yards of sticky tape

Staples

Large plant pots

Side windows from wrecked autos

Two miles of safety pins and rubber tubing

Garden cane

Fuel tank from old Ford Pinto

Bulldog clips

Hairy string and bailing wire

Expendable people

Whitewashed corrugated scrap iron

Doors from old barn

TOTAL COST OF PROJECT: $750.00
SHUTTLE PROJECT BUDGET: $345,000,000,000
MISCELLANEOUS EXPENDITURE REF ICA HOLDINGS: $344,000,000,250

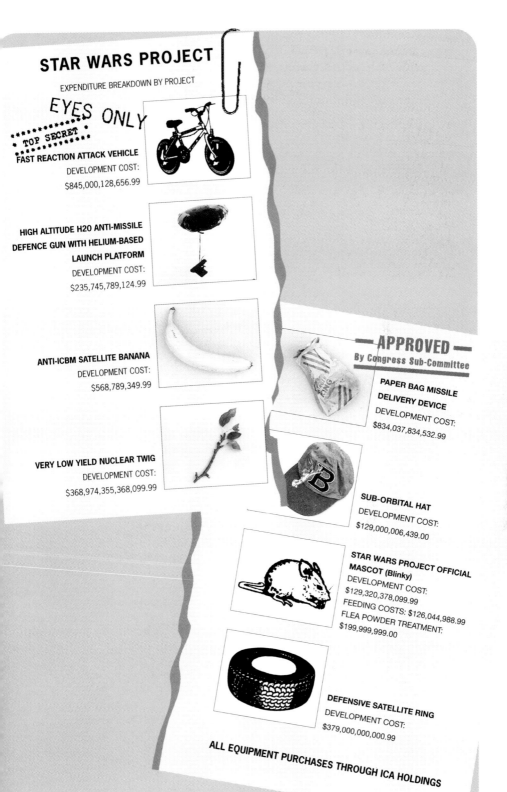

STAR WARS PROJECT

EXPENDITURE BREAKDOWN BY PROJECT

FAST REACTION ATTACK VEHICLE
DEVELOPMENT COST:
$845,000,128,656.99

**HIGH ALTITUDE H20 ANTI-MISSILE
DEFENCE GUN WITH HELIUM-BASED
LAUNCH PLATFORM**
DEVELOPMENT COST:
$235,745,789,124.99

ANTI-ICBM SATELLITE BANANA
DEVELOPMENT COST:
$568,789,349.99

VERY LOW YIELD NUCLEAR TWIG
DEVELOPMENT COST:
$368,974,355,368,099.99

— APPROVED —
By Congress Sub-Committee

**PAPER BAG MISSILE
DELIVERY DEVICE**
DEVELOPMENT COST:
$834,037,834,532.99

SUB-ORBITAL HAT
DEVELOPMENT COST:
$129,000,006,439.00

**STAR WARS PROJECT OFFICIAL
MASCOT (Blinky)**
DEVELOPMENT COST:
$129,320,378,099.99
FEEDING COSTS: $126,044,988.99
FLEA POWDER TREATMENT:
$199,999,999.00

DEFENSIVE SATELLITE RING
DEVELOPMENT COST:
$379,000,000,000.99

ALL EQUIPMENT PURCHASES THROUGH ICA HOLDINGS

TRANSCRIPT FROM NSA AUDIO SURVEILLANCE OPERATION:
LOCATION: BASEMENT, FBI BUILDING

AGENT MULDER: The Space Shuttle cost less than a thousand dollars to cobble together. The Star Wars programme was a complete fake. Where's the money really going, Scully?

AGENT SCULLY: Maybe the money's going to so-called 'Black Projects', Mulder, unofficial government programmes they can't reveal to Congress. Look, both reports talk of funds going to ICA Holdings. Mulder, what do you get if you rearrange those letters?

AGENT MULDER: ACI - the last Pharaoh of sunken Atlantis? Of course! It's so obvious!

AGENT SCULLY: You're really not at your best before your tenth cup of coffee of the day, are you? C-I-A. Mulder, the money's going to the CIA!

X-FILE X-72365
COMPUTER REF: BLACK TIES
REPORT BY AGENT FOX MULDER
EYES ONLY

Once I gave The Lone Gunmen the name of ICA Holdings, it only took Byers some five minutes to hack into company records and download a series of reports on secret CIA 'Black Projects'.

This is how taxpayers' money is really spent...

CENTRAL INTELLIGENCE AGENCY
Washington 25 DC

* TOP SECRET *

PROJECT: HEAVEN CAN'T WAIT
FINAL REPORT

CANCELLED

PROJECT: Using the very latest cryogenic techniques, our plan is to 'deep freeze' a CIA operative and drop his body temperature down to the point where his heart stops. His soul will then leave his body and travel to Heaven, where he will talk to God. We will then slowly revive him and he will provide any intelligence gleaned during the mission.

PROJECTED SCENARIO:

AGENT: Great. It worked. I'm dead.

ST. PETER: Welcome to Heaven. Now, if you might just...

AGENT: Shut it, Heaven-Boy! I'm here to see the big chief...

GOD: It's all right, Peter. He's with the CIA. Let him approach my throne.

AGENT: Good morning, God. CIA. I'd like to ask you a few questions.

GOD: Sure, go right ahead. As a loyal American, it's my duty to co-operate with the CIA.

AGENT: Glad you see it that way. Now, you're omniscient, right?

GOD: I see everything that ever was, is, or shall be.

AGENT: So, you know where the Russian subs are.

GOD: Oh yes.

AGENT: And you know the location of all their missile silos?

GOD: Of course, I can see the smallest feather on the tiniest sparrow in the farthest reaches of my Kingdom, so a big bastard like an SS-20 ICBM is no problem...

AGENT: I want those details.

GOD: You got 'em! Me bless America!

ACTUAL OUTCOME: Every agent who 'went over' resigned and subsequently went into a monastery.

REASONS FOR CANCELLATION: CIA Agents, apparently, don't go to *Heaven* when they die...

TOP SECRET

CENTRAL INTELLIGENCE AGENCY
Washington 25 DC

CODE NAME: ROOM WITH A VIEW
FINAL REPORT

CANCELLED

PROJECT: People with proven psychic ability are placed in a room and asked to 'see' what Russian leaders are doing by a process known as 'Remote Viewing'.

TYPICAL RESULT:

CONTROL: Can you see anything?

VIEWER: Can I? Oh boy! Yeah! Wow! Whahoo! Go baby go! Look at them legs!

CONTROL: That's not Boris Yeltsin you're looking at, is it?

VIEWER: Oh, eh, yeah. Sure it is. Best legs in Moscow, that premier. All right! Off it comes. Yes! Shake those tomales! Er - I mean, sign that document!

CONTROL: It's Pamela Anderson's bedroom. You're back in Pamela Anderson's bedroom again, aren't you?

VIEWER: Yeah, all right. So what? I just can't help it. I keep thinking about her and...I see...

CONTROL: Concentrate on Yeltsin!

VIEWER: Sure...OK, there he is - oh dear, he's drinking again. Yup, that's what he's doing all right...

CONTROL: You're making it up. You're still in Pamela Anderson's bedroom!

(Pause)

CONTROL: What's she wearing?

VIEWER: Ab-sol-utely nothing...

CONTROL: Wow! Draw us a picture!

REASONS FOR CANCELLATION: Pamela Anderson.

CENTRAL INTELLIGENCE AGENCY
Washington 25 DC

CANCELLED

CODE NAME: YETI BOY CASTRO
FINAL REPORT

PROJECT: To turn Cuban President Fidel Castro into a Yeti.

PROPOSED METHOD: To arrange for the president either to be bitten by a Yeti or to receive a massive blood transfusion from one.

REASONS FOR CANCELLATION: We couldn't find a Yeti.

SEE ALSO: PROJECT BIGFOOT, PROJECT VAMPIRE, PROJECT MUMMY, PROJECT WEREWOLF, PROJECT NESSIE.

CENTRAL INTELLIGENCE AGENCY
Washington 25 DC

CODE NAME: TIN CAN
FINAL REPORT

CANCELLED

PROJECT: To have Cuban President Fidel Castro's brain removed and put inside a thirty foot tall killer robot.

REASONS FOR CANCELLATION: We couldn't remember why we thought this was a good idea in the first place...

CENTRAL INTELLIGENCE AGENCY
Washington 25 DC

CODE NAME: SQUISH
FINAL REPORT

CANCELLED

PROJECT: To have Cuban President Fidel Castro's brain removed and jump up and down on it.

REASONS FOR CANCELLATION: Failure to secure President Castro's brain...

CENTRAL INTELLIGENCE AGENCY
Washington 25 DC

TOP SECRET

CODE NAME: RAQUEL
FINAL REPORT

CANCELLED

PROJECT: To subject Raquel Welch to mind-altering techniques (cf: MK - ULTRA) and then get her to come on over to my house while my wife's out and sit on me.

REASONS FOR CANCELLATION: Agent who proposed idea fired with full loss of pension.

CENTRAL INTELLIGENCE AGENCY
Washington 25 DC

TOP SECRET

CODE NAME: RED SPLODGE
FINAL REPORT

CANCELLED

PROJECT: A satellite orbiting the earth would track and monitor the movement of Mikhail Gorbachev by identifying the birthmark on top of his head. This would enable his location to be constantly monitored and, at a given command, an earth-launched ICBM could be accurately targeted to within 6 feet of his forehead.

REASONS FOR CANCELLATION: In trials, the satellite had serious difficulties in distinguishing between Gorbachev's birthmark and the British mainland. Failure to correct this error might have resulted in an international incident.
    Plus, he sometimes wore a hat, or went indoors.

CENTRAL INTELLIGENCE AGENCY
Washington 25 DC

TOP SECRET

CODE NAME: LOUD AND CLEAR
FINAL REPORT

CANCELLED

PROJECT: To shout President Fidel Castro.

ACTIVITY: At 7.00 am on Friday 15th June 1979, 157 Field agents spread throughout the nation all shouted President Fidel Castro's name for a period of some ten minutes at the top of their voices.

REASONS FOR CANCELLATION: It was all an embarrassing typing error...

While Byers was exploring the covert CIA funding, he turned up something unexpected - a parallel account feeding huge sums of money in and out of a single Savings and Loans account, the owner of which was only identified by a mobile phone number. If parts of the government were raising and distributing funds in this way, Congress would never ever get to know of it. It looked suspiciously like Byers had stumbled on to something even bigger still. I decide to give the number a call...

TRANSCRIPT FROM NSA AUDIO SURVEILLANCE OPERATION:
LOCATION: BASEMENT, FBI BUILDING

BLEEPING SOUND OF TELEPHONE

AGENT MULDER: Hello? I'm in the market.

VOICE: Yo! Hold it, bro'! This mobile shit ain't secure. Doctor C be ringing you back, Jack, on my secure line. Where you at, homes?

AGENT MULDER: 555-3456

CLICK

AGENT MULDER: Scully, get this line tapped...

SOUND OF PHONE RINGING

AGENT MULDER: Hello?

VOICE: Yo. Wassup?

AGENT MULDER: Er...I want to talk to 'Doctor C'.

VOICE: You got him. Like they be sayin', 'Dr C, LSD, Reefer, Crack an' nose candy!'

AGENT MULDER: I'm looking to get fixed up....

VOICE: My main bitch, Hillary, gonna come straight over with Doc C's magic medicine, make you feel all right! Courtesy o' Doctor C! Give the ho the dough for the blow, Joe.

AGENT MULDER: I'm not a user. I'm - a businessman. I want 14 kilos of pure cocaine. Can you handle that kind of weight?

VOICE: Yo. Why d'yall think they call the White House 'The White House'?

AGENT MULDER: I always thought it was just a racist thing.

AGENT SCULLY: Mulder...you're not going to believe this...

AGENT MULDER: Hold on, Scully...Hey, Doc C, we gotta meet?

VOICE: The Alley. 14th an' main. Half an hour. Bring the cash. Half an hour...

AGENT SCULLY: Mulder...

AGENT MULDER: Did you trace the call?

AGENT SCULLY: Mulder...that call came from inside The White House.

AGENT MULDER: *Doc C*...it couldn't be, could it Scully?

Scully and I attended the meet.

It was a trap.

As we waited, a speeding government car approached. As it got closer, the window in the back came open. They were going for a drive-by hit. In a split second, I saw the Uzi come up and heard someone shouting, 'Yo! Muthas! This is for you!' As I pushed Scully to the ground and glanced up, I thought I recognised the shooter as none other than Vice President Al Gore. The driver could have been Secretary of Defence William Perry, but I didn't get a clear look.

Bullets rattled all around us. We drew our guns, but before we could return fire the car had sped off again.

I know one thing. They've lost my vote.

As we picked ourselves up, X emerged from the shadows. 'Still sticking your nose where it's not wanted, Agent Mulder?' he asked. 'Drop it! It's too big for you. They will crush you like an ant!' He then handed me a sealed manilla envelope. I then tried to ask him why he kept telling me to drop all my investigations and then gave me things that made me start them up again, but he had already disappeared back into the darkness, where he had trodden in something, judging from the disapproving noises I could hear him making...

I took the envelope back to the office. I was not prepared for what I found inside...

Operation 'Nowhere To Run'

NOVEMBER 1970

Today, the world is plagued by seemingly insoluble problems such as over-population, declining food supplies, global pollution, the threat of nuclear war, new diseases, ozone depletion and drought.

This discussion paper explores a number of radical alternatives to ensure the survival of the American nation - or at least the parts of it that matter. We are fully aware that it is only possible to have two alternatives in a strictly grammatical sense, but we needed to reach for Alternative 3 - and beyond...

Alternative 1
Cure all diseases, control the elements to avert natural catastrophes, invent a viable alternative to the internal combustion engine, make farming 75% more productive and enforce a unilateral ban on all nuclear weapons.
Probability of success: 0%

Alternative 2
Build huge subterranean cities powered by hordes of mind-controlled slaves operating a giant treadmill to generate electricity.
Probability of success: 38%

Alternative 3
Build secret bases on the moon and fill them with just the ruling elite.
Probability of success: 65%

Alternative 4
Build a miniaturising ray gun and shrink the whole of America's population to a tiny, tiny size just like they did to Kandor, the city in a glass bottle, in *Superman*.
Probability of success: 12%

Alternative 5
Put everyone in cryogenic suspension for 55,000 years by which time

pollution would have had time to disperse and the next Ice Age would have come and gone.
Probability of success: 4%

Alternative 6
Build a teleportation ray like they have in *Star Trek* and beam everyone to a lovely new planet that's just like earth but with none of the problems.
Probability of success: 8%

Alternative 7
Build a giant space ark out of gopher wood and titanium alloy and fill it with everyone in America (except the poor) and animals two by two (except the smelly and dangerous ones, and the ones that don't taste nice). Launch it into space and find a nice new planet to live on.
Probability of success: 25%

Alternative 8
Kill all the poor people so that the natural resources last longer for those of us left.
Probability of success: 45%

Alternative 9
Implant everyone's brains into indestructible robots that don't need to eat and can survive radiation.
Probability of success: 30%

Alternative 10
Saw mainland America off from the bedrock, cover it in a huge airtight dome and then attach giant rocket motors to California and Florida, powered by the oil reserves under Texas. Go off exploring the Galaxy.
Probability of success: 2%

Alternative 11
Open up a gateway into a parallel world which has not been spoiled. Go there and start again. When that world is spoiled, move to the next dimension.
Probability of success: 4%

Alternative 12
Invent a very very big time machine, go back and kill off all the dinosaurs and then relocate all American citizens to the Jurassic period.
Probability of success: 2%

Like everyone else, I had heard of 'Alternative 3', but always thought it was government disinformation. Could government drug deals really be financing secret luxury bases on the Moon? It sounded eerily plausible.

I asked Frohike. His answer was no, rather disappointingly...

He told me that we had never even reached the Moon, let alone secretly colonised it, and the evidence he had amassed from friends inside NASA to support his theory was pretty convincing...

BUD's MODEL MART
GRAND PLAZA SHOPPING MALL, HOUSTON, TEXAS

To: NASA Mission Control

Date: 7th January 1969

Items:		
1 model Revell Saturn V	$ 4.20
1 model Lunar Module	$ 2.40
1 model Service/Command Module	$ 3.40
2 tubes polystyrene cement	$ .80
1 lunar globe	$ 8.00
1 world globe	$15.00
1 ball string	$ .65

CENTRE STAGE COSTUME HIRE
2342 Allende Road, Houston, Texas

To: NASA Mission Control

Date: 6th January 1969

Items:
Two 'I Dream of Jeannie' spacesuits
c/w helmets, backpacks and boots
(1 week hire): $80.00

HOAGLAND QUARRIES
Piper Road, Houston, Texas

To: NASA Mission Control

Date: 16th January 1969

Items: 2 tons assorted rocks
and boulders
                    $826.00

'FLORIBUNDA'
LANDSCAPE GARDENERS
2661 Saint Quentin Drive,
Houston, Texas

'Lunar Landscapes a Specialty'

To: NASA Mission Control
Date: 12th January 1969

Items:
To design and build an authentic lunar landscape
'Sea of Tranquility' region $18,358.00
Extra for star backdrop: $ 1,520.00

(Joe, quote for Mars landscape to follow)

You may not need us very often - but you'll be glad we're there when you do!

Finally, most damning of all, Frohike had managed to get hold of a transcript of an audio tape created in a sound studio in Hollywood...

Aldrin: That's one small step for mankind...

Producer: Cut! Buzz, baby. That's 'small step for man' - not 'mankind'.

Aldrin: Sorry Larry.

Producer: OK people. Let's take it from the top. Take two...

Aldrin: That's one small step for mankind...shit!

Producer: Cut! Don't worry Buzz. Take three...

Aldrin: That's one small step for man, one giant sleep...

Producer: Cut! That's 'giant leap' - not 'giant sleep'.

Aldrin: OK Larry. Sorry. All these people on the set are making me a bit nervous. I'll be all right.

Woof! Woof!

Pres. Nixon: Fetch the ball, Checkers...

Producer: Places everyone. Take four...hold it. Mr President, could you please be just a teeny-weeny bit quieter? Thank you. OK everyone, take four...

Pres. Nixon: I'm not making any noise and I'm not the President. I'm Tippi Hedren. And that's not my dog. It's JFK's kangaroo.

Producer: As you say, Mr President. Now, action!

Aldrin: That's one small step for man, one giant leap for man.

Producer: Cut! Buzz, Buzz. You're nearly there. It's 'giant leap for mankind'.

Aldrin: OK. OK. I think I've got it.

Producer: All right. Take number five...we're rolling.

Aldrin: That's one small step for man, one giant leap for... for... what's that word again?

Producer: Cut! Cut! Buzz. It's no good. We're just wasting time here. Armstrong! Come down off that ladder and change places with Buzz.

Have we never reached our closest neighbour, or do we have vast cities peopled by the elite on her sunless surface even now? Is the President a drug baron, raising money for his insidious schemes?

Assistant Director Skinner has just entered my office so I'm going to turn off my computer and go home now, because I don't want to get sent for therapy again.

MONSTERS FROM THE VATS

The definition of the X-Files on which FBI Agents Mulder and Scully worked was actually far more broad than an investigation into our activities here.

It also, for example, covered the investigation of strange creatures. From time to time, we created bizarre new monsters in the gene vats and released them to keep Mulder and Scully busy and away from the core purpose of their investigations.

Some of our earlier creations, like Bjork, were laughed off by the FBI. Other early attempts, like a very rubbery humanoid called Tooms who could squeeze into confined spaces, were equally silly but more effective in wasting FBI time. As we became more experienced, our creature program became a genuine thorn in Agent Mulder's side...

X-FILE X-71182
COMPUTER REF: TUT, TUT.
REPORT BY AGENT FOX MULDER
EYES ONLY

CONCLUSION:
It's not my fault. *It was a mummy* that was killing the museum curators. And it had bandages trailing behind it and it did have its arms outstretched and it did say 'woo-ooo-ooo, you have awoken me from my 5000-year-old slumber and invoked the Curse of Ra'.

I am not mad. Scully saw it too. Almost. She was just in the other room, but had she been in the same room there was no way she could have missed it.

I do not need another week in therapy or one of the orange pills they give out there.

X-FILE X-71221
COMPUTER REF: A QUICK BITE
REPORT BY AGENT FOX MULDER
EYES ONLY

CONCLUSION:

When Scully and I checked out his motel room, he really had registered as 'Count Alucard'. Really. You can go to the motel. Look at the guest books. It's there, and I didn't put it there.

I agree that the sun dissolving his bones to a fine powder which then blew away out of sight of everybody but me is 'unsatisfactory' in validating my report, but that's what happened.

X-FILE: X-71651
COMPUTER REF: PURPLE PEOPLE
EATERS
REPORT BY AGENT FOX MULDER
EYES ONLY

CONCLUSION:

It was an easy mistake to make. Anyone could - and would - have made it. I don't deserve suspension and I don't deserve the cruel sneers and jibes from my fellow agents when I go to the canteen.

The creature had eaten God knows how many kids from here to California. All the eyewitnesses agreed. It was some kind of reptile with big teeth, standing about seven feet tall on its rear legs with mauve scales and a green-spotted back.

I had to take it out before anyone else got hurt...

COMPLETE STOCKS

WEDNESDAY

EXTRA EDITION

LATE SPORT

NEW YORK DAILY NEWS

VOL XC   SIX PARTS – PART ONE   WEDNESDAY MORNING, 10TH JULY, 1996   92 PAGES   DAILY 75c

TV'S BARNEY GUNNED DOWN BY FBI

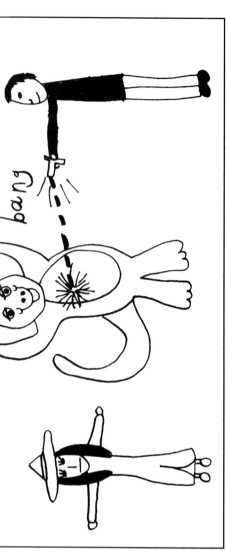

bang

Barney the TV Dinosaur was gunned down by the FBI yesterday in a bizarre and tragic case of mistaken identity.

'I accidentally mistook him for another seven foot purple dinosaur,' said FBI Special Agent Fox Mulder, 35, the man who fired the fateful shot with his 9mm Smith and Wesson 1056.

Millions, many of them children, watched live on television as the deadly drama unfolded.

Barney was just showing the children some of the wonders of Mexican culture, such as how to

I STILL LOVE YOU, SAYS BARNEY

out of a neighbour's hubcaps and the Hispanic lyrics to the traditional Mexican song 'Welfare Check, Welfare Check, Aye, Aye, Aye!', when Agent Mulder burst into the recording studio in Connecticut.

'I was scared when the man bursted in,' said Barney's 'very special friend' Peter, aged 7½. 'He shouted for Barney to move away from us kids and not to eat us. Barney said that he loved kids and then the man shot his gun and Barney made a funny high pitched sound and fell backwards onto my friend Conchita and made her cry.'

Luckily, the bullet fired by Agent Mulder's gun hit a piece of gold genital jewellery being worn by the actor inside the costume and glanced away. No one was hurt by the ricochet.

Barney was immediately rushed to the nearby hospital, where he was set upon by gleeful children from the paediatric ward and later needed treatment for hug-related injuries.

Agent Mulder was arrested at the scene by local law enforcement officers but later released pending possible disciplinary proceedings.

Barney's shooting has led to charges of a government shoot-to-kill policy against popular children's favourites by right wing pressure groups. 'They wanted the dinosaur silenced,' said Ubergruppenfuhrer Bob Bobsley of the 'Right To Shoot People Coalition', 'because he's anti centralised government. When they attacked Waco, it wasn't David Koresh they were after, it was Fozzie Bear!' He then wet himself and had to go and change.

Special Agent Mulder was also reported to have been hurt in the incident after being bitten on the ankle by Barney's 'Very Special Friend' Jeremy, aged 5.

Agent Mulder is no stranger to controversial shooting incidents in bizarre circumstances. Last month, he winged Sesame Street's Big Bird in a separate shooting. He later claimed to have been searching for the 'Thunderbird' flying creature of Indian legend.

'I love you all,' said TV's Barney last night, recovering in a Connecticut hospital bed. 'even you, Mr FBI Man – because the police are our friends and we must love them!' Barney said he had even composed a special song which went, 'Me love you, you love I, we all love the FBI'

Our reporter made his excuses and left.

LATEST

MICKEY IN GUN HORROR

'GIANT MUTANT RAT' SAYS FBI GUNMAN HELD AT SCENE.

'I don't know what to say,' said FBI Spokesman Assistant Director Walter S Skinner last night, 'I'm sorry. Sometimes he's a complete asshole...'

However, sometimes, the monsters in the human imagination can prove more destructive, and more terrible, than anything we might create in the gene vats...

Today, Scully and I were given the strangest X-File duty of all. Skinner came by and assigned Scully and myself to...babysitting duties. It seems his little niece and nephew are staying with him and he's been called out of town on urgent FBI business.

TRANSCRIPT FROM NSA SURVEILLANCE. RE: MELISSA SCULLY (DECEASED) SECOND BEDROOM, RESIDENCE OF ASSISTANT DIRECTOR SKINNER, FBI.

TAMMI: Tell us a story, Uncle Mulder.

BENJI: Yes! Tell us a story, unca Mulder!

AGENT MULDER: Sure, on July 3rd 1947, in the New Mexico town of Roswell...

AGENT SCULLY: I don't think that's a suitable story, Mulder...

TAMMI: I like stories about ponies!

AGENT MULDER: Well, there was this horse called Snippy who was abducted by a flying saucer in the 1960s. When his carcass was discovered all the blood...

AGENT SCULLY: Mulder!

BENJI: Did a monster get him?

TAMMI: Monsters don't really exist, do they, Auntie Scully?

AGENT SCULLY: Of course not. Now you try and get some sleep...

AGENT MULDER: They do.

AGENT SCULLY: They don't.

AGENT MULDER: Kid, I've seen vampires, werewolves, demons, witches, killer slugs that jump down your throat, dead convicts coming back from the grave...

TAMMI: Waaaaa!

AGENT SCULLY: Ignore the bad man.

TAMMI: Sob...We're scared, Auntie Scully.

BENJI: Yeah, - sniffle - the bogieman might get us. He might come out of that closet and...

AGENT SCULLY: Mulder! Put the gun away!

AGENT MULDER: You heard what the kid said, Scully. There's a monster in the closet!

TAMMI: Waaaaaaaaa!

BENJI: Waaaaaaaaa!

AGENT SCULLY: It's OK. Uncle Mulder is only joking. He doesn't really think the bogeyman is in the closet.

TAMMI: Sob-sob-It's OK now?

AGENT SCULLY: Yes, I promise...

BENJI: It is - sob - all right, isn't it, Unca Mulder? Sniffle-sniffle.

AGENT MULDER: Kid, it's never all right. When I was younger, the aliens came in the middle of the night and snatched my little sister for horrible medical experiments.

TAMMI: Waaaaaaaaa!

BENJI: Waaaaaaaaa!

X-FILE 396599
COMPUTER REF: THE LITTLE PEOPLE
REPORT BY AGENT FOX MULDER
EYES ONLY

I am pleased to report that everything's on the mend now. The doctors say that Tammi will only need to be in therapy for another six months - tops - and her straps have been loosened. Benji is well on the way to cutting back on his chronic bedwetting episodes and recognises both his parents. Both can now talk again.

My jaw has healed and Skinner is finally controlled enough not to leap at me and pummel me whenever we pass in the corridor.

Perhaps we hide too much from children. Or perhaps, as adults, we know too much. Our parents hid the truth from us. There *are* monsters out there. I will never again know the precious, innocent and comforting sleep of childhood - but at least I can buy X-rated videos, so I guess it's a fair trade-off.

INSIDE THE WHITE HOUSE

X-FILE: X-77824
COMPUTER REF: WEREWOLF IN THE
WHITE HOUSE
REPORT BY AGENT FOX MULDER
EYES ONLY

Following our case 'The Jersey Devil' (cf: X-File X-71231) about a cluster of 'man-beasts' discovered living in the New Jersey woods, and our discovery of lycanthropes on a remote Indian reservation in Browning, Montana (cf: X-File X-77300, 'Shapes'), I have searched FBI files to see whether these were isolated cases, or whether we are facing an epidemic of lycanthropic behaviour.

To my surprise, cases bearing a distinct similarity occurred in Arkansas from 1989–1991 and right here in Washington DC from 1992 to the present.

In each case people walking through or near thick undergrowth at night were attacked by a wild beast, which left dog-like bite marks. Witnesses have said that the creature was half human and howled like a wolf.

What worries me is not that we might have a werewolf to track down, but given that the attacks in Arkansas and Washington were identical – down to the bite marks – I have every reason to believe that this werewolf is President Clinton...

I have decided to pursue this investigation myself before involving Scully since I want to be certain of my facts.

THE WHITE HOUSE PRESS OFFICE
WASHINGTON

With Compliments

Dear Special Agent Mulder,

Thank you for you letter of November 12th. You are quite correct in stating that President Clinton did not attend any public engagements on July 15th, August 14th, September 12th, October 12th or November 11th which are, as you state, dates of the full moon.

If we can be of any further assistance please let us know.

THE WHITE HOUSE PRESS OFFICE
WASHINGTON

With Compliments

Dear Special Agent Mulder,

Thank you once again for your recent enquiry. According to the police files, Vincent Foster, Financial Advisor to the Clintons, committed suicide in June 1993. As far as I know he was not 'Savagely slain because he knew too much about the President and his lycanthropic tendencies'.

With Compliments

Dear Special Agent Mulder,

To the best of my knowledge, neither President Clinton nor any member of his entourage has ever been found naked in the wolves' enclosure at Washington Zoo in the early morning. If he does, I will be the first to inform you.

THE WHITE HOUSE PRESS OFFICE
WASHINGTON

With Compliments

Dear Special Agent Mulder,

Hillary Clinton has asked me to inform you that her health care reforms do not include a proposal for federal funds to be allocated to finding a cure for lycanthropy. I am sorry if this is not the answer you were hoping for.

THE WHITE HOUSE PRESS OFFICE
WASHINGTON

With Compliments

Dear Special Agent Mulder,

President Clinton has asked me to inform you that, yes, his favourite meat is lamb - but that he does not 'devour live sheep and leave their partially eaten bodies and entrails littering the White House lawn'.

THE WHITE HOUSE PRESS OFFICE
WASHINGTON

With Compliments

Dear Special Agent Mulder,

I can confirm that our cleaning staff did discover tufts of moulted fur on the carpet of the Oval Office but this was attributed to Socks and not a 'half-man, half-beast' that you imply.

THE WHITE HOUSE PRESS OFFICE
WASHINGTON

With Compliments

Dear Special Agent Mulder,

I can confirm that 'strange howls' were reported two weeks ago from President Clinton's quarters but this was nothing more than his usual Wednesday night saxophone practice.

THE WHITE HOUSE PRESS OFFICE
WASHINGTON

With Compliments

Dear Special Agent Mulder,

The corridors of the White House are kept spotlessly clean by our janatorial staff and they would have certainly reported finding something like 'Stop me before I kill again' daubed in fresh blood on the walls.

THE WHITE HOUSE PRESS OFFICE
WASHINGTON

With Compliments

Dear Special Agent Mulder,

You are correct in saying that Socks the cat did disappear for two days last week but she had gone on a goodwill tour of Southern States and was not as you suggested, 'eaten by the President in an uncontrollable blood-lust'.

I believe you have been misinformed once again.

THE WHITE HOUSE PRESS OFFICE
WASHINGTON

With Compliments

Dear Special Agent Mulder,

For your information, the 'Whitewater' affair did concern the Clintons'
involvement in Arkansas real estate but the property did not include a 500 acre
wolf sanctuary.

THE WHITE HOUSE PRESS OFFICE
WASHINGTON

With Compliments

Dear Special Agent Mulder,

President Clinton has asked me to point out that although he does quite like
A Company of Wolves, Frankenstein Meets The Wolfman, An American Werewolf In
London, The Howling and The Jungle Book, he does not count any of them among
his top films of all time - and has certainly not played a 'significant cameo
role' in any of them.
I hope this answers your question and believe that no useful purpose would be
served by pursuing this line of enquiry any further.

THE WHITE HOUSE PRESS OFFICE
WASHINGTON

With Compliments

Dear Special Agent Mulder,

Questions about scratchmarks on Hillary Clinton's back are not the remit of this
office.
   Cease and desist all further correspondence with this office...

**TRANSCRIPT OF NSA SURVEILLANCE OPERATION
LOCATION: OFFICE OF ASSISTANT DIRECTOR WALTER S SKINNER,
FBI BUILDING**

ASSISTANT DIRECTOR SKINNER: I've been reading your latest X-File report with interest, Agent Mulder.

AGENT MULDER: Thank you, Sir. I...

ASSISTANT DIRECTOR SKINNER: So you believe that President Clinton is a werewolf.

AGENT MULDER: Yes sir. I...

ASSISTANT DIRECTOR SKINNER: Let me just get my file. Ah yes. Last month you said he was Dracula, Agent Mulder. Before that he was a drug baron, and before that he killed Kennedy - and Buddy Holly. He's been a dupe of the aliens, Nixon's love child, Godzilla, Bigfoot, Springheeled Jack, my clone, your clone, Scully's clone, a clone of a clone, a loaf of bread, Jack the Ripper, Satan, Satan's clone, Amelia Earhart, Amelia Earhart's love child and Amelia Earhart's clone.

He kidnapped the Lindbergh baby. He perpetrated the Zodiac Slayings. He started World War One. He was lead singer with The Doors. He invented Ebola. He uses witchcraft to fix the Superbowl. He keeps Elvis in a cupboard.

AGENT MULDER: All right. I've been wrong in the past, but the evidence this time...

ASSISTANT DIRECTOR SKINNER: Mulder! I don't want to hear it! Having a lead is one thing but having an obsession is another! You've been acting irrationally lately and that's no good for you and no good for the Bureau. I covered your butt after the Barney shootings and, before that, your attack on Big Bird, but enough's enough. I was hauled over the coals by the Director over your actions at Disneyland and our lawyers tell me that a large out-of-court settlement is inevitable. We're trying to keep it out of the papers but I'm not gonna take the rap this time.

Mulder, I've closed down the X-Files before and I won't hesitate to do it again. You know your remit, and this does not, I repeat *not,* involve harassing the President of the United States, wasting your time, but more importantly – my time, into the bargain!

Now get out of here before I ask for your badge.

AGENT MULDER: But Sir, this time...

ASSISTANT DIRECTOR SKINNER: I don't want to hear it Mulder. Take a break. Go away somewhere. Anywhere. Out of state. You've been working too hard. Agent Scully will cover for you. I'll see you in a few days.

Skinner knew. He knew Clinton was a werewolf, but his hands were tied. Someone was pulling strings behind the scenes.

If anyone was going to take Clinton down, it would have to be me...

TRANSCRIPT OF NSA SURVEILLANCE OPERATION
LOCATION: OVAL OFFICE, THE WHITE HOUSE, WASHINGTON DC

KNOCKING

PRESIDENT CLINTON: Enter...

AGENT MULDER: Mr President? Special Agent Fox Mulder, FBI.

PRESIDENT CLINTON: Bill Clinton, President. Now, what's this all about?

AGENT MULDER: I've good reason to believe there's a mass murderer loose in the White House, Sir.

PRESIDENT CLINTON: And you thought you'd come straight to me? You know, your voice is awfully familiar. Have we met before?

AGENT MULDER: These are for you.

PRESIDENT CLINTON: You bought me some flowers?

AGENT MULDER: Yes. Wolfsbane. Here, take a closer look. A very close look!

PRESIDENT CLINTON: They're lovely. I'll put them in a vase.

AGENT MULDER: Oh. I also bought you this, Sir.

PRESIDENT CLINTON: A huge chunk of raw bloody steak? I'm very grateful but - you're dripping blood on the carpet.

AGENT MULDER: Does it get your pulse racing, Sir? Do you feel the pull of the deep, dark woods? Is your blood afire?

PRESIDENT CLINTON: I like steak, yes...

AGENT MULDER: I thought you would. That's why I also brought this...

PRESIDENT CLINTON: Agent Mulder, why are you pointing your gun at me?

AGENT MULDER: This is loaded with bullets...silver bullets, Mr President. I have good reason to believe you are a werewolf, Sir. Le Loup Garou.

PRESIDENT CLINTON: Is this *Candid Camera*?

AGENT MULDER: When the moon comes up, and you change, I will stop your rampage of terror forever...

PRESIDENT CLINTON: Surely you wouldn't shoot the President of the United States?

AGENT MULDER: I think you'll find it's a great American tradition, Sir.

PRESIDENT CLINTON: I am not a werewolf. Are you mad? How can I convince you?

AGENT MULDER: Well, in five minutes the moon will have risen, Mr President. The full moon - but you already knew that, didn't you? Then we'll know the truth. You can't hide your transformation. Perhaps then, you'll feel like eating me. Sinking your fangs into this succulent flesh...

PRESIDENT CLINTON: Agent Mulder, why are you taking your clothes off? Someone might come past the window and look in...

AGENT MULDER: When the transformation comes, you won't be able to resist me...

PRESIDENT CLINTON: Why...why are you rubbing that lotion all over you?

AGENT MULDER: It's garlic butter. It wards off evil. Bite me and you die...

PRESIDENT CLINTON: You're crazy...

AGENT MULDER: Now you take *your* clothes off, Mr President.

PRESIDENT CLINTON: What?

AGENT MULDER: You heard. All of them, Sir. Now.

PRESIDENT CLINTON: Yeah. OK. Don't shoot. Look, there was a mix up with my underwear this morning. I was in such a rush to get to the office that I accidentally put on Hillary's. I don't usually...I just don't, OK?

AGENT MULDER: When you start to turn into a wolf, I'll spot it immediately.

PRESIDENT CLINTON: I'm not going to turn into a wolf, Agent Mulder.

AGENT MULDER: Yeah, just like you didn't inhale...

LONG, BLOOD-CURDLING HOWL FROM *OUTSIDE* THE BUILDING

ANXIOUS SHOUTS AND THE SOUND OF RUNNING

AGENT MULDER: Oh.

PRESIDENT CLINTON: You see?

LONG, BLOOD-CURDLING HOWL FROM *OUTSIDE* THE BUILDING

AGENT MULDER: Don't worry, Sir. I'll protect you from it.

PRESIDENT CLINTON: But who's going to protect me from you?

AGENT MULDER: Oh my God! Out the Oval Office window! That shadowy canine shape...

SOUND OF GUNSHOT

PRESIDENT CLINTON: That's Secretary of Defence Perry's spaniel, Tufty, you just shot, you mad bastard...

SOUND OF VIOLENT SCUFFLE

AGENT MULDER: Get off me! Get off my back, Mr President!

PRESIDENT CLINTON: You...stupid...bastard!

MORE VIOLENT SCUFFLING

DOOR BURSTS OPEN. FIVE FBI BODYGUARDS ARE HEARD TO ENTER

BODYGUARD 1: We heard the shot, Mr President. Are you...oh my God!

BODYGUARD 2: That's Fox Mulder from VCU! Jesus, 'Spooky' Mulder's slipping it to the President...I knew he was odd...

BODYGUARD 3: Oh, er, we'll um...come back when you're not busy. Sorry, Mr President...

PRESIDENT CLINTON: It's not what it looks like...

BODYGUARD 1: Whatever you say, Mr President. I never saw you naked and wrestling another naked man all oiled up on the Oval Office carpet. No Sir. It won't be in my report, Sir.

PRESIDENT CLINTON: Get out all of you - and take this man with you. He's insane. Completely crazy...

MULDER IS ESCORTED OUT UNDER ARMED GUARD

LONG, BLOOD-CURDLING HOWL FROM OUTSIDE THE BUILDING

SOUND OF PHONE BEING DIALLED

PRESIDENT CLINTON: Hillary? We got a problem. I think Chelsea's broken out of her enclosure again...

X-FILE: X-77824

COMPUTER REF: WEREWOLF IN THE
WHITE HOUSE

SUPPLEMENTARY REPORT BY AGENT
DANA SCULLY

EYES ONLY

I thought of visiting Mulder in the Bureau Sanitarium, but Skinner says that Mulder needs a complete rest.

Because of the embarrassing circumstances under which Mulder was apprehended, the whole incident has been officially 'forgotten' and no mention of it will go in Mulder's File.

I blame myself. I should have seen this coming. Mulder sets impossible demands on himself and a complete mental and physical breakdown like this was long overdue. When he returns, I shall try to be more supportive.

SPACE CATS

TRANSCRIPT FROM NSA SURVEILLANCE OPERATION:
LOCATION: BASEMENT, FBI BUILDING

AGENT SCULLY: Welcome back, stranger! It hasn't been the same without you...

AGENT MULDER: Scully...?

AGENT SCULLY: Yes?

AGENT MULDER: They locked me up, Scully.

AGENT SCULLY: I know Mulder. I - I'm sorry. How are you feeling now?

AGENT MULDER: I've had a lot of time to think, Scully - and I think I've made a breakthrough...You know the typical representation of a Gray?

AGENT SCULLY: What about it?

AGENT MULDER: Do you notice anything odd about the eyes?

AGENT SCULLY: Why? What are you talking about?

AGENT MULDER: Scully, I'm serious. I think I'm on to something. Take a look at this drawing of a Gray. Do you think it's got the same sort of eyes as a cat?

AGENT SCULLY: Pardon me?

AGENT MULDER: See. If I cover up the forehead, mouth and cheeks - you could be looking at a cat...

AGENT SCULLY: Oh Mulder, three months of ECT for nothing...

AGENT MULDER: I'm fine, Scully. Really. It's all here. In these books...

AGENT SCULLY: These ones? The Erich von Daniken ones? The ones he wrote that no one took seriously? The ones that didn't sell...

AGENT MULDER: They're rather interesting, Scully. I had plenty of time to study them. Lots of time...I know them by heart.

AGENT SCULLY: Mulder, this man believed that cats made the Nazca lines in Peru with their claws and they were actually landing strips for spacecraft carrying fresh supplies of milk...

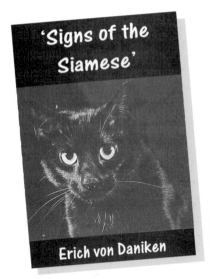

'Signs of the Siamese'

Erich von Daniken

'In Search Of Ancient Tabbies'

Erich von Daniken

'Catnip of the Gods'

Erich von Daniken

'Miracles of the Moggies'

Erich von Daniken

'Return to the Litter Box'

Erich von Daniken

'Chariots of the Pussies'

Erich von Daniken

Some of von Daniken's later and more obscure works dealing with his theory that in the earth's remote past, the planet was visited by a race of cats from another galaxy, who perhaps fathered humanity.

AGENT MULDER: Yes, he did...

AGENT SCULLY: Mulder, this man claimed that star cats carved those mysterious statues on Easter Island and left suddenly because their supply of fish disappeared...

AGENT MULDER: Hmm, interesting, isn't it...

AGENT SCULLY: Mulder, this man seriously believed that a highly evolved race of tabbies built the Great Pyramid of Cheops, teleporting the stone blocks that weighed thousands of tons just by twitching their magic whiskers?

AGENT MULDER: So far, so good...

AGENT SCULLY: Oh Mulder, it's *The Lion, The Witch and The Wardrobe* all over again...

AGENT MULDER: Narnia is out there Scully. It's just a question of finding the right wardrobe...Von Daniken was right, Scully, but he didn't go far enough...Listen to this, *Hey Diddle, Diddle...*

AGENT SCULLY: That's it. I'm off to the canteen. Do you want a bap?

AGENT MULDER: The cow was levitated 'over the moon', Scully. It was abducted. And there's a cat in the rhyme and a dish. A dish, Scully. A saucer! Why was the cow abducted?

AGENT SCULLY: Mulder, we solved that. It was a crazed bunch of cow worshippers in Wyoming...

AGENT MULDER: That's what *they* wanted us to think, Scully. UFOs are abducting cows - for the milk. For the cats on board. It all makes sense...

AGENT SCULLY: Maybe you came out a bit early.

AGENT MULDER: I've had so much time to think about it, Scully! Cats look like Grays because they come from the same planet. They're in it together, Grays and Cats. Cats and Grays. Scully...Look at this Viking I photograph of Mars. See...you just add a few lines and it all becomes so clear. Scully, there's a cat's face on Mars...

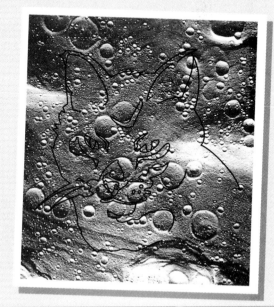

Scully is no longer talking to me. She has taken her work and her houseplant and gone to work out in the corridor. Every so often, I see strange distorted faces pressed up against the glass in my office partition, and anxious-sounding voices. I don't care.

I'm finally making significant headway...

Following standard FBI procedure I pulled a suspect in for questioning - the first cat I found.

I started off by trying to win the creature's trust as best I could. This I did by behaving in a similar fashion: crouching down on all fours and miaowing, rubbing myself against my desk and purring and climbing on to the top shelf and licking myself clean. Unfortunately I slipped during the last manoeuvre and knocked myself out.

Shortly after coming to I began the telepathy experiments. Sadly, these proved no more successful. She steadfastly ignored the Zenner cards and, as she did not pick up the pen, I have no way of knowing if she received the mental pictures of my sister that I was attempting to transmit...

I tried hypnotic recall on the cat earlier, utilising a simple pendulum, but she kept batting it with her paw so I gave up.

I have, however, made one breakthrough. I have learned the cat's name. (This was relatively easy, because it was on a little disc attached to her collar.)

By now I realised that the cat was not going to share any secrets with me so I decided to let her go. I hoped she'd lead me straight to her Gray co-conspirators so, following from a discreet

distance, I tailed her into the alley two blocks away behind the local Chinese restaurant... Now I know her rendezvous site with the Grays, I can set up a stakeout...

GINGIE
081963742

Public enemy number one

X-FILE X-79999 "CATS"

Day 10 — or is it 11 — of my stake out. I am still sequestered in the alley, wearing my cat-suit. The back-up I requested has still not arrived.
Looks like I'm on my own - again.
There is still no sign of the Grays.
I am putting all the experience I gained in profiling serial killers to good use here. In Quantico, they taught me that, to understand a killer you have to think like one. Out here, in the alley, I am gaining a deeper understanding of cats. I forage like them for scraps in the bin, sit on the fence and sing all night. I chase the rats. I run away from stray dogs - and all the while I watch ... and wait. They will come. And they will lead me to my sister.
Last night, I thought the Grays had arrived, but it was only some Chinese chef from the restaurant putting out the trash. I was disappointed, but dined like a king.
They will come ...

TRANSCRIPT FROM NSA SURVEILLANCE OPERATION
ALLEY OF 14TH AND 7TH, WASHINGTON, DC.

AGENT SCULLY: He's over here, sir...

ASSISTANT DIRECTOR SKINNER: Mulder...Fox. You've got to come with us now...

AGENT MULDER: Miaow.

ASSISTANT DIRECTOR SKINNER: That's right. That's all right. You've done a good job, Agent Mulder. Time to come in now...

AGENT MULDER: Miaow.

AGENT SCULLY: Oh...Mulder...

ASSISTANT DIRECTOR SKINNER: You take one arm, I'll take the other. Come on Fox...

X-File.
By Special Agent Fox Mulder.

Scully came to visit me today. She brought
me flowers. They were delicious.
 I asked her when I could come home and
she started to cry.
 Skinner offered her my job but she said no.
She doesn't believe.
 I still believe.
The truth is out there.
It's just a pity that I'm in here...